Some Issues in Nyāya, Mīmāṁsā and Dharmaśāstra

Sri Garib Das Oriental Series No.—197

Some Issues in Nyāya, Mīmāṁsā and Dharmaśāstra

Ujjwala Panse

Sri Satguru Publications
A Division of
Indian Books Centre
Delhi - 110007

Published by :
Sri Satguru Publications
Indological and Oriental Publishers
A Division of
Indian Books Centre
40/5, Shakti Nagar,
Delhi-110007
(INDIA)

First Edition: Delhi, 1996

ISBN 81-7030-477-6

Printed at:
D.K. Fine Arts Press (P.) Ltd. Delhi

Printed in India

अज्ञानतिमिरान्धस्य ज्ञानाञ्जनशलाकया।
चक्षुरुन्मीलितं येन तस्मै श्रीगुरवे नमः।।

श्रियः प्रदुग्धे विपदो रुणद्धि
यशांसि सूते मलिनं प्रमार्ष्टि।
संस्कारशौचेन परं पुनीते
शुद्धा हि बुद्धिः किल कामधेनुः।।

Foreword

I am happy to associate myself with this Publication of a young Scholar Dr Ujjwala Panse by way of this brief foreword. Dr Panse is already known to the Academic Circle through her Research volume i.e., 'A Reconstruction of the Third School of Pūrvamimamsā'. That work was her Doctorate thesis. Normally the Doctorate thesis should be the beginning of one's research career. However, in many cases it becomes the end of it. Dr Panse has proved that there are a few serious young scholars who carry forward the research on the issues briefly touched in their thesis. The present volume constitutes the result of such an endeaver.

In this volume Dr Panse has dealt with sixteen topics. Three of these are the issues of Nyāya. Nine are the issues of Pūrvamimamsā and four relate to the interesting areas of Dharmaśāstra. Excepting the last two, the other issues are in a way continuations of her earlier research in her doctoral thesis.

We rarely have a modern Scholar who is well versed both in Nyāya and Mimāmsā. Dr Panse has the advantage of fairly good grounding in both. This is clear from the topics selected by her and the method of treatment of these topics.

Let me illustrate it by her treatment of one or two topics. In her essay on 'Is *Anuvyavasāya* a *Laukika pratyakṣa*?' She raises the question whether it is *Mānasa pratyakṣa* as held by *Prāchinanyāya* or *Jñnalakṣṇā pratyāsattijanya pratyakṣa* in the case of external objects as held by Navīnanyāya. She explains the procedure of contact of senses, the object, and the knowledge according to both the views and comes to the conclusion that in the view of Navīnayāya it is *laukika* so far as the internal objects are concerned and *Alukika* in the case of external objects. For *Prāchinayāya* it is *laukika* in both the cases. She has made a lucid analysis of the relevant textual passages.

The concept of *Anuvyavasāya* is not accepted by Bhātta and Prābhākara Mimāṁsā and also by Vedānta. They have managed the role of *Anuvyavasāya* by *Jñātatā, Svaprakāśatva, Sākshi* and such other devices. It will be a worthful enquiry if the study of the different views in Indian Philosophy in respect of this concept of Anuvyasāya is made.

Within the Nyāya frame work also one or two questions may be raised and enquired. In the instances of *Jnānalakṣaṇā pratyāsatti janya jñāna* such as *'Surabhi Chandanam' Sourabhya* is provided as additional content by *Jñāna lakṣaṇā pratyāsatti*. But in the case of *Anuvyavasāya* the content i.e. external object of the *Vyavasāya* and *Anuvyavasāya* is the same. Its nature is explained as 'Anuvyavasāyatvañcha Vyavasāyaprakāra prakārakatayā tatprakāravadviśeṣyakatayā cha a tadviṣayaka pratyakṣatvam'

अनुव्यवसायत्वं च व्यवसायप्रकारकतया
तत्प्रकारकवद्विशेष्यकतया च तद्विषयकप्रत्यक्षत्वम्

The similarity between *Jñānalaksaṇā pratyāsatti janyajñāna* and *Anuvyavasāya* is only in respect of a previous knowledge providing the content to a later knowledge. However, in the case of *jñanalakṣaṇā pratyāsatti* the knowledge obtained by the eye i.e. the knowledge of *Chandana* is provided with an additional content Saurabhya while in the case of Vyavasāya providing the content for Anyvyavasāya, what is obtained by the sense as the content at the stage of Vyavasāya is passed on to Anuvyavasāya as its content. Therefore, it has to be examined whether it is worthwhile to treat it on par with *jñānalakṣaṇā pratyāsatti*. Further, to treat it as *laukika pratyakṣa* in the case of internal objects and Alaukika in the case of external objects will introduce a dichotomy.

In the context svatastva or Paratastva of Prāmāṇa also the question whether Anuvyavasāya comprehends only Rajatatva prakarakatva or comprehends Rajatatvaviśiṣṭatva is raised in Tattvachintāmaṇi and it is remarked that Rajatatvavaiśiṣtya being external Anuvyavasāya cannot cover it. Dr Panse may take up some of these intricate issues and probe further into this concept. It will be a good contribution to Indian Epistemology.

In the essay on 'Murāri Misra on Kārya and Siddha' Dr Panse brings out an interesting point that the scope of Kārya as conceived by Murāri is wider than that of Prabhākara. She states that within the scope of Kārya, Murāri brings the *niyojya* also. She quotes Murāri's statement '*Kṛtyanurañjanayogyam kāryam atra abhipretam*' and contrasts it with the Śālikanātha's statement *Kṛti Sādhyam Kāryam*.

The concept of Kārya is an important concept in Prabhākara. It is the import of a Vedic injunction. It is designated by three names viz., *Apūrva*, *Niyoga* and *Kārya*. It is called *Apūrva*, because, it is not conveyed by any other Pramāṇa other than Vedic injuction i.e., Mānāntarāpūrva. It is called *Niyoga* as it commands a Niyojya and it is called Kārya as it implies a duty. The Bhāṭṭa concept of Apūrva is different from Prabhākara's concept of Apūrva. Kārya has to be distinguished from Kriyā. The Kriyā is viṣaya as well as karaṇa of Kārya. Prābhākaras do not seek a Bhāvya or Sādhya out side the Kārya. A vedic injunction conveys Kārya as connected with Niyojya and viṣaya. The role assigned to Arthavāda by Bhāṭṭas is rejected by Śālikanatha. However, he does not make it clear as to what role is assigned to Arthavāda by Prabhākara and how it is connected with Kārya. Therefore, Dr Panse's finding of the role assigned by Murāri Miśra and his bringing it within the scope of Kārya is quite interesting. She may trace further observations of Murari on this point so that we may get a full idea of Arthavāda's position vis-a-vis Kārya. She may also check up Bṛhatī on Arthavādādhikaraṇa.

In the essay on 'Tantra and Avāpa', Dr Panse takes another interesting issue. Here, she discusses the ground on which Tantra and Prasaṅga are to be distinguished. With her fascination for Murāri She states that Murāri makes the ground of this distinction more clear by offering a number of explanations of the nature of Tantra than Bhāṣyakāra or Vāritikakara. She quotes about four explanations of Murāri. This gives us a clear idea of Tantra and Prasaṅga.

Mīmāṁsā has made distinct contribution in two areas: (1) Interpretation of the scripture (2) Organisation of ritual programme. The first has resulted in a comprehensive study of the language in general and the second has resulted in the study of the programme organisation in general i.e., the management of the programmes in general.

In formulating the guidelines for the ortganisation of the ritual programme on programmes in general they have taken into account

(i) The efficiency
(ii) The economy of efforts

(iii) The result oriented approach
(iv) Elemination of subjective bias and wasteful items and wasteful procedures.

The three items discussed in this essay viz., Tantra, Avāpa and Prasaṅga are the devices that are intended to achieve i) economoy of effort and ii) Efficiency.

In Śābara Bhāṣya, Śabara gives the examples of implementing these devices both in respect of ritual programmes and day to day life.

For instance, in the ritual programme of Darśapūrnamāsa whether in respect of Agneya and Agniṣomiya, the Agent, the place and the time should be the same or different is settled in favour of 'the same'. Similarly whether Agnyādhāna be made for each sacrifice separately or the Agnyādhāna once made be utilised for all sacrifices is settled in favour of one. Whether, sacrificial instruments Sruk, Sruva etc., prepared for the first time be utilised for the later sacrifices also or each time a separate set be prepared is settled in favour of 'One set'. These are ritual instances of Tantra. From day to day life also Śabara gives interesting examples. When the villagers of a village are asked to dig a well whether each one should dig a separate well or they should jointly dig one well, naturally will elicit the answer that they should jointly dig one well. This is an example of Tantra in day to day life. Similar examples both from the ritual area and day to day life area are given for Avāpa and Prasaṅga also.

The common feature of Tantra and Prasaṅga is that both serve more than one. The distinguishing feature is that while Tantra is intended to serve all those that it serves, the Prasaṅga is intended to serve only one but its serving the others is incidental.

(i) *Sakṛtkṛtam bahūnām upakāri Tantram* सकृत-कृतं बहूनामुपकारितन्त्रम्

(ii) *Anyopakārārtham Kṛtena anyasya upakāra siddhiḥ Prasaṅgaḥ* अन्योपकारार्थं कृतेन अन्यस्य उपकारसिद्धिः प्रसङ्गः

These two explanations explain the role of Tantra and Prasaṅga respectively. However, their distinction is made clear in the remark.

(iii) *Tantram anekopakorakamapi tāvaduddeśena anuṣṭhānamiti Prasaṅgataḥ tasy bhedaḥ* तन्त्रम् अनेकोपकारमपि तावदुद्देशेन अनुष्ठानमिति प्रसङ्गतो तस्य भेदः।

Śabara himself has made this distinction clear by quoting a verse 'Sādhāraṇam bhavet tantram' etc.

Dr Panse has presented this distinction very clearly quoting the statements of Murāri also.

In view of her correct grasp of these devices of programme organisation if she collects all the examples of day to day life given by Śabara and the other Mīmāṁā writers and brings the relevance of these guidelines for modern programme management, it will be a very useful contribution.

Mīmāṁsā contribution to the legal interpretation is already brought to the notice of the modern Academic world. Mīmāṁsā contribution to the programme management also needs to be brought to the notice of modern Academic world.

The last four topics viz., Women and Omen etc. handled by Dr Panse do not belong to the area of my study. However, they are very relevant contemporary topics. Many Scholars of Sociology and the activist of Social reforms are writing volumes on Woman without a deep study of Dharmaśāstra and the other relevant literature, picking up a few quotations here and there. Therefore, it is necessary that the Scholars who have full access to Dharmaśāstra literature take up this study and make an objective assessment of Indian thought on 'Woman'. One or two such objective studies are made by the Western Indologist where seminars on 'Gender' are frequently organised.

'The perfect Wife: The orthodox Hindu Woman according to the *Strīdharma paddhati* of Tryambaka Yajvan' by Dr. Julia Leslie is one such study. *Dharmākūtam* a commentary on Rāmāyaṇa by Tryambaka Rāya Makhin also presents the entire Hindu Dharma Śāstra thought on 'Woman'. An objective study along with a field work of the present thought and actualities is worth undertaking.

I feel that the foreword has become a little elaborate than what normally is expected of a foreword. However, with a view to bring out the importance of the topics discussed here and also highlight the pains taken by Dr Panse in handling such highly technical issues, I had to write a little elaborately.

I congratulate Dr Panse for her very useful contribution to the Indian Philosophical thought.

DARŚANRATNA, MIMAṀSĀ BHŪṢAṆA

K.T. PANDURANGI
Formerly Professor of Sanskri,
Bangalore University
Upakulapati, Poornaprajna Vidyapeetha.

Acknowledgement

I feel happy to put on record the names of persons to whom I owe this book. First and foremost among them is my husband Prof. V.N. Jha, from whom I learnt the ABC of Nyāya and Mīmāṁsā. He always inspires me by his tremendous capacity to work and taking everything to be secondary to academic activity.

My mother who is now only in my memory, always loved and appreciated my academic achievements. My father and elder brother have always been encouraging me in my research activity. I am grateful to them. It is my good fortune that I was born in such a cultured and loving family.

I also thank the staff of the library of the Centre of Advanced Study in Sanskrit, Poona University and that of the Bhandarkar Oriental Research Institute, Pune for their cooperation and help.

I am very grateful to Prof. Pandurangi for blessing me by writing a foreword for this book. I shall try my best to pursue research in the direction and areas that he has suggested.

I am thankful to all those who directly or indirectly have helped me in bringing out this work.

Lastly, I thank the publishers for showing keen interest in printing this book.

Ujjwala Panse

Contents

Abbreviations

ABORI	Annals of Bhandarkar Oriental Research Institute
Asv.gr.	Aśvalayanagṛhyasūtra
Av	Atharvaveda
Bhā	Bhāṭṭas
BHU	Benares Hindu University
BORI	Bhandarkar Oriental Research Institute
CIIL	Central Institute of Indian Languages
Comm	Commentary
Ed	Edited/Editor
JORM	Journal of Oriental Research, Madras
JS	Jaimini Sūtras
Kau gr.	Kauṣitakigṛhya Sūtra
KS	Kauśikasūtra
MS	Maitrāyaṇī Saṁhitā
Ms	Manuscript
NM	Nyāyamañjarī
p	page
PM	Pūrvamīmāṁsā
PP	Prakaraṇapañcikā
P_p	Pūrvapakṣa/Pūrvapakṣin
pp	Pages
Prā	Prābhākaras
Ṛv	Ṛgveda
ṢaḍBr	Ṣaḍviṁśa Brāhmaṇa
ŚBh	Śābarabhāṣya
ŚBr	Śatapatha Brāhmaṇa
TC	Tattvacintāmaṇi
Tr	Translation
TS	Taittiriya Samhitā
Vol.	Volume
VS	Viṣṇu Smṛti
YS	Yājñavalkya Smṛti.

Introduction

This book is an outcome of some of my research work of last few years. I worked on the Third School of Pūrvamimāṁsā i.e. the School of M.M. Murāri Miśra, for my Doctorate. The thesis is published under the name, "A Reconstruction of the Third School of Pūrvamimāṁsā" in 1990 by Sri Satguru Publications, New Delhi.

Thereafter I concentrated on the remaining works of Murāri which I could not incorporate in my thesis due to the fear of making it very bulky. Simultaneously, I studied some Nyāya texts and also some of Dharmaśāstra, both being the fields of my interest along with the Mimāṁsā System of Indian Philosophy. Thus, this small work consists of some studies in Nyāya some in mimāṁsā and also a few in Dharmaśāstra.

The first chapter deals with Jayanta Bhaṭṭa's concept of the Relation between Word and Meaning. In this, the reader will find a case where Jayanta is in total agreement with the tradition. He has followed the steps of Gautama, Vātsyāyana and Udyotakara wholeheartedly and has elaborated their opinions from all possible ways. He has refuted the stand of mimāṁsakas in a very systematic way. To explain, he has taken all the arguments that Śabara has made while commenting upon Jaimini's sūtra 1.1.5, into consideration and has answered them all in his own poetic language.

The next issue is that of *Anuvyavasāya*. *Anuvyavasāya* is nothing but an awareness of perceptual cognition. The problem is how is it produced? This has been discussed in the system right from the time of Vātsyāyana, the commentator of *Nyāyasūtras* c Gautama. While commenting upon his *Bhāṣya*, Vācaspati Miśra ii his *Tātparyaṭīkā* on Udyotakara's *Nyāyavārtika* has accepted *anuvyavasāya* to be a mental perception. Now it can be mental perception if and only if the mind has the capacity to perceive internal objects as well as external ones and if it is so then one may argue that there is no necessity of the external sense-organs like eyes etc. Because if mind perceives the external objects also then there is no function left to perform for the external sense-organs like eyes etc. To overrule this contingency, Vācaspati argues, in keeping with the line of Bhāṣya, that though *anuvyavasāya* is a category of mere mental perception still there is a role for the external sense-organs to play. What is that role? The role is to produce *vyavasāya* i.e. the object of *anuvyavasāya*. To explain if the opponent's view be right that in the presence of mind all external sense-organs remain jobless then there will be a contingency, in turn, that there will be no categories of blind, deaf, etc. as they also have their internal sense-organ namely mind intact. But the fact is that they do not have *anuvyavasāya* like 'I see the pot' or 'I hear of a pot', respectively. And hence it is necessary that the external sense-organ should produce the *vyavasāya* namely perception of a particular object based on which will follow the awareness of that perception i.e. *anuvyavasāya*.

This is how Vācaspati has discussed the issue. Praśastapāda in his *Padārthadharmasaṅgraha* simply says that the qualities of the soul namely *buddhi* etc. are known by the contact between mind and soul. Śrīdhara in his *Nyāyakandali* over the above line of Praśastapāda clarifies that knowledge etc. are known by the contact *saṁyuktasamavāya*. Well, this is accepted by all. But there is something which needs our careful consideration. And this is discussed in the issue Is *Anuvyavasāya Laukika Pratyakṣa*?

The next issue discusses the definition of *pratyakṣa* stated by Viśvanātha in his *Nyāyasiddhāntamuktāvali*. Naiyāyikas have accepted two types of soul - *jīvātman* and *paramātman*. Jīvātmā is *kiñcijjña* and *paramātmā* is *sarvajña*. The knowledge of jivātman is a product whereas the knowledge of the *paramātman* i.e. God is eternal i.e. *nitya*. Viśvanātha has given a definition which is applicable to both the *jīvapratyakṣa* as well as to the *īśvarapratyakṣa*. It is this definition of *pratyakṣa* given by Viśvanātha which is common to both the *Jīvapratyakṣa* and the *īśvarapratyakṣa* that is discussed in this chapter : "A Note on Viśvanātha's Definition of Pratyakṣa".

The following chapter entitled "Murāri on Validity of Knowledge" discusses how Murāri Miśra's view on Validity of knowledge is different from the other two schools of *Pūrvamīmāṁsā*.

The theories of the Bhāṭṭa School of *Pūrvamīmāṁsa* and the Prābhākara School have also been summarised in this Chapter.

The point to be noted is this : Sources to know the Doctrine of Murāri Miśra, the founder of the Third School of Pūrvamimāṁsā are scanty. They are : a few fragments of his works and references to his doctrine by other authors. His view on validity of knowledge has not been attested in any of his own works today available to us. But this view is referred to by various philosophical texts, Whosoever refers to Murāri Miśra, he ought to refer to his independent doctrine regarding the validity of knowledge. It is only through these references we come to understand his theory of Validity of Knowledge - and it is the very first thing that separates him from other two schools of Pūrvamimāṁsā, and from any other system of Indian philosophy for that matter. As I have said already elsewhere that there are many a topic where he is either very much influenced by the Prābhākara doctrine or he has freely borrowed from Prābhākara texts but still one should not get confused and identify him as a follower of Prabhākara as the views held by Murāri are, certainly not identical with that of Prābhākara's on certain topics. The foremost of such topics is the one of validity of Knowledge, I have shown the exact position of Murāri from the sources that are attested in various texts, mainly the Nyāya texts.

The next issue is that of the concepts of qualifier and indicator.

These two concepts are actually same so far as their function namely distinguishing something from something else is concerned but they are different so far as their nature is concerned. I have tried to take a survey into the history and development of these two concepts. So far as these two are concerned, Murāri has been influenced by the Prābhākara stand obviously. He has defined these two Concepts in the terminology common to that of Prabhākara and his followers. Nevertheless he has maintained his independent identity by denying the established way of defining these concepts. He has defined these two by avoiding the usage of the term distinguisher or differentiator i.e. *vyāvartaka* or *avacehedaka* as was done by almost every philosopher before him.

The reason that he gave for this is that differentiating or distinguishing something from the other or others is the function performed by both of these concepts alike. And hence that need not occupy any place in the body of the definition, as definition should be something which is a unique property of the definitum, (There is an interesting and elaborate discussion about the definition of definition in the *Tarkadīpikā* which is a self-written commentary on *Tarkasaṅgraha* of Annambhaṭṭa)

Thus, here also he has proven his distinguished position. The following issue is that of the intention of the speaker : *Tātparya*. The context is this : Verbal understanding is an understanding that arises from the knowledge of a sentence (of a reliable speaker.). While understanding the sentence-meaning does one have to know the intention of the speaker or does verbal understanding arise even in the absence of knowledge of the intention of the speaker. This is the issue. Answer to this question is not unequivocal so far as the mīmāṁsakas and the Naiyāyikas are concerned. I have tried to highlight the reason behind their peculiar stands in this chapter.

The next issue deals with the concept of *kārya* as accepted by the Prābhākaras. This article is mainly based on the *Prakaraṇapañcikā* of Śālikanātha. It is true that for the Prābhākaras *kārya* stands for *apūrva* i.e. the merit produced by the sacrifice. But this meaning of *kārya* is restricted to the vedic texts and not to our day-to-day behaviour. He says so far as our *Laukika vyavahāra* is concerned, *kārya* is nothing more than an action.

"A note on Prābhākara Theory of *Śābdabodha*" is the following chapter - Prābhākara Theory of *Śābdabodha* is known by the name *anvitābhidhānavāda*. Their stand is that a word does not denote its meaning in isolation from an action. The meaning of a word is always to be understood in connection with some action. In other words, a word will not convey any meaning if the sentence is actionless.

I have tried to specify the ares of application of this theory-in this chapter. The method put forward by the Prābhākaras is nothing but the direct method (in today's terminology) of learning a language. This method is adopted by a child when it first learns a language. There is no doubt that this direct method is the most effective means of learning language. Wherever a language is learnt by following the direct method in all those cases the Prābhākara Theory of verbal understanding is applied. In case of first language learning i.e. by a small kid this is the sole method that is used by the child universally. But even in the cases of second or third language learning if the direct method is used then there the *anvitābhibhāna* theory alone works that is what the Prābhākaras plead for.

But one should remember that direct method be it the most effective one is not the only technique to learn a language. Other theories such a *abhihitānvayavāda* or *saṁsargamaryādāvāda* of the Bhāṭṭas and the Naiyāyikas respectively, do equally matter, so far as the second onwards language learning is concerned. Nevertheless, Prābhākara's Theory alone is applied by a child and never or very seldom the other theories. Similarly this theory is the most effective one even in other cases.

The following topic "Prābhākaras on Negation" is again based mainly on *Prakaraṇapañcikā* of Śālikanātha. In this chapter I have tried to specify the verbal understanding arising out of a sentence containing a negative particle according to Prābhākaras. As the Prābhākaras do not accept absence as an entity there is no referent to the word *na* or any negative particle for that matter. This is the foremost objection of the opponents against Prābhākaras that what and how will a person understand a sentence containing any negative particle. Following the foot-steps of Śālikanātha, I have tried to make his intention as transperent as possible, and have tried to pinpoint the verbal understanding as it would look like.

Comparing Prābhākaras position and terminology I feel that he has borrowed the terminology from the Buddhists. If we compare him with Dharmakīrti (see the definition of in *Nyāyabindu*) it becomes obvious that he has borrowed his terminology but has built his own theory on the basis of it.

The chapter "On Editing Murāri Miśra" describes how I have tried to edit Murāri's *Arthavādādhikaraṇa*. Editing any of Murāri Miśra's works is a sort of difficult endeavour as there is no help to the editor left in the form of more manuscripts or even some commentary on any of his works. Hence one has to depend solely on one's knowledge of the system of Pūrvamīmāṁsā, of Logic and Philosophical framework of the system etc. Still I have made an attempt in this direction. In this chapter I have given a few cases where I required to edit the text to get the coherent meaning from it.

The following chapter discusses the peculiar definitions offered by Murāri of the concepts of *kārya* and *siddha* in his *Arthavādādhikaraṇa*. By defining the concept of *kārya* the way he has defined it what he has achieved is that he could include *niyojya* in the class of *kārya*.

Though, his terminology shows close similarity with the Prābhākara system in general and Rāmānuja in particular, there is no doubt about the fact that Prābhākaras would never treat *niyojya* as *kārya*. I have elaborately described and compared both the stands i.e. that of Murāri and that of Prābhākaras.

Tantra and Āvāpa are the two concepts Murāri Miśra has discussed in his *Ekādaśādyādhikaraṇa*. These two are technical terms. *Tantra* is a performance which helps many simultaneously and hence needs no repetition. Whereas, *āvāpa* is a performance which is performed as many times it is enjoined by different injunctions.

Murāri has discussed various definitions of *tantra* and has given his own definition at the end. Āvāpa is not a very controversial concept and hence there is not much that he has to say on it either. This is discussed at length in the chapter Murāri on *Tantra* and *Āvāpa*.

The following chapter is : Omens : Past and Present. Omens is an interesting topic in the history of human civilization. In this chapter I have tried to search for the oldest record of the concept. In the Ṛgveda, i.e. the oldest historical literature, there are two hymns devoted to this some omens which are believed in even today.

"Attitude and Feelings of man towards Nature as Reflected in Dharmagranthas" speaks for its contents itself. It was an amusing exercise to look into these texts and find out their awareness about our natural wealth and its protection. A reader will also find it interesting I am sure.

The last two chapters are also interesting ones as they deal with the position of women. Freedom of women was, is and will be the topic of importance and interest so long as there are male dominated civilizations.

I have tried to understand Manu's possible attitudes by reading between the lines sometimes and mainly by reading apparent contradictory rules together.

In the last chapter namely, Duties of Women in the Yājñavalkya Smṛti, I have discussed the matter confining my self to the Yājñavalkya Smṛti only. I have taken relevant verses from the Smṛti and have tried to understand the mind of the seer in this context.

If scholars in the respective fields find the issues raised in this book interesting, I shall consider my efforts rewarded.

Gaṇeśa Caturthī **Ujjwala Panse**
29-8-1995.

1

Jayanta on the Relation Between Word and Meaning

0.0. *Naiyāyikas* from the time of Gautama have two prominent opponents in addition to the Buddhists namely, the *Vaiśeṣikas* and the *Mīmāṁsakas* so far as verbal testimony as a means of valid congnition is concerned. Three controversial aspects of the issue are :

(1) Whether verbal testimony is an independent means of valid congnition, (2) Whether there is any relation between a word and its meaning and (3) What is the nature of that relation i.e. whether it is an eternal one or otherwise?

As we know, *Vaiśeṣikas* do not accept that verbal testimony is an independent means of valid congnition; they include the same in the inference. Buddhists did not accept that there is any relation between word and meaning. Similarly, *Mīmāṁsakas* held that the relation between the two is eternal.

In this paper we are mainly concerned with the last controversy.

0.1. Presuppositions

(1) Verbal Testimony is a means of valid cognition,
(2) There is a relation between a word and its meaning, and
(3) The knowledge of this relation is necessary for verbal understanding. In other words, the knowledge of the relation between word and meaning is necessary for verbal testimony to play the role of a means of valid cognition.

With these presuppositions in mind we shall now first see what Jayanta has to say on the relation between word and meaning, in his *Nyāyamañjarī* (*NM*).

0.1. Jayanta on *Pada-padārtha-sambandha*

At the very outset Jayanta declares that unless there is a relation between a word and its meaning in the form of *samaya* i.e. convention formed by somebody (*puruṣa*) a word does not produce an understanding of the meaning. (पुरुषपरिघटितसमयसम्बन्धव्यतिरेकेण शब्दादर्थप्रत्ययानुत्पत्तेः। सम्बन्धकरणे पुरुषानपेक्षत्वम् अघटमानम् NM p. 220)

Thereafter he begins the discussions at the very beginning, and states that the relation between a word and its meaning cannot either be *saṁyoga* like that between a pot and berry or *samavāya* like that between a cloth and threads because we do not perceive it. Neither can it be inferred because we do not experience the cutting of or filling up of mouth with sweets as soon as the words like *kṣura* (knife) or *modaka* (sweets) are uttered. Since the word exists in mouth and the referent on earth there is no invariable concomitance or co-locus-ness between the two.

The relations like *kāryakāraṇabhāva, nimittanaimittikabhāva* or *ādhārādheyabhāva* are not possible in case of these two, but we cannot also say that there is no relation at all between them as word is the reason of the regular understanding of certain meaning. *NM*, p. 221) But the relation is also not of the nature of *hetu-hetumad-bhāva*. Then what is the nature of that relation? The relation, Jayanta states is called *samaya* and it is defined as : *abhidhāna abhidheya—niyama—niyogaḥ samayaḥ* (*NM*, P. 221) which means : Convention of the regularity between a word and a meaning. If one asks what is the exact nature of this *samaya* then Jayanta answers it is actually nothing but *saṁjñā—saṁjñi—sambandha* of the *Mīmāṁsakas*. Unless this *samaya* is known the nature of a word as a revealer is not understood and hence, he adds, the relation between the word and the meaning is not natural. In other words, words do not possess any natural power or capacity that denotes their meanings (*NM*, p. 223)

1.1. Thus, to sum up the stand of Jayanta:

(1) There is a relation between the two.
(2) That is named as *samaya*.
(3) This *samaya* is defined by Jayanta as : *abhidhāna-abhidheya-niyama-niyoga* which means : regular application of the

consistent relation between word and meaning, which ultimately may take the form of desire be it of the God or of the man.

(4) Unless this *samaya* is known verbal understanding will not take place.

From this it seems to me that, this *samaya* is nothing but what is later called *saṁketa* and *lakṣaṇā*, or *śakti* or *vṛtti* by the later authors on *Navya-Nyāya* like Gadādhara, Viśvanātha etc.

Nature of the *saṁketa* is, as Gadādhara states : the desire of God or that of man that may be expressed in words as : Let this word denote this particular meaning or let this meaning be understood from this particular word. (vide *Śaktivāda*, pp. 15)

Let us now look at the stand of the *Mīmāṁsakas* in brief and then see how Jayanta has answered them.

2.0. Mīmāṁsakas Position

(1) Words possess a natural power / capacity (*śakti*) to denote meanings and it is known through the behaviour of elderly persons. This power of words is as natural as the power of burning in the fire and hence there is no concern of a human being so far as the relation between word and meaning is concerned.

(2) Knowledge of this natural relation is necessary for knowing the meaning just as the natural property existing in smoke, namely, *analāvinābhāvitva* has to be known for an inferential cognition. In other words as inferential cognition of fire does not arise unless you know the relation between smoke and fire so also verbal understanding does not take place unless the relation—be it natural—is known.

(3) All words are capable of expressing all meanings. This explains different meanings of the same word in different regions.

2.1. Jayanta's Answer to Mimāṁsakas

Jayanta refutes all these arguments one by one and does not accept that the relation is eternal or natural.

(1) Natural relation cannot be accepted because, as we

perceive the words and meanings we do not perceive any third entity namely the relation between them. If *Mīmāṁsakas* intend that this relation being of the nature of a capacity or potentiality in words cannot be perceived separately, then this capacity which is different from the nature of a thing has already been refuted by Jayanta on the ground that it is not perceptible because it is not a substance. It is not inferable because effects come into existence even otherwise. And most important is, even if this relation between word and meaning in the form of capacity among words is accepted, still one cannot do away with *samaya*, because unless *samaya* is known one cannot understand the meaning (of a word). Thus, one has to accept *samaya* on the top of the natural power and it is already established how *samaya* itself is sufficient to make one understand the meaning, then why unnecessarily should one go for the natural relation between the two?

(2) On the second argument of the *Mīmāṁsakas* which explained the necessity of the knowledge of the natural relation between a word and a meaning by giving an analogy of smoke and fire, Jayanta says, this argument is not sound because though *analāvinābhāvitva* (i.e. the state of not existing without fire) is natural to *dhūma* its *pratyāyakatva* (i.e. the state of being a revealer) is not natural and hence unless we know it no inferential knowledge of fire is possible but in the present context the *Mīmāṁsakas* contention is that the capacity to denote the meaning (*pratītiśaktiḥ*) i.e. *pratyāyakatva* or capacity to reveal itself is natural to the word then why on earth is there any necessity of knowing the relation?

(3) The third point that all words denote all meanings is also difficult to accept because it is not possible to differentiate among different *śaktis* of a word—because the *śakti* is nothing but the nature of the word itself. One cannot infer this *śakti* on the basis of the difference in the effects because that difference can be explained even otherwise. Moreover, if all *śaktis* are present in one and all words then all meanings will be understood from any word. Here, if one says that the knowledge of *samaya* will come

for help then Jayanta says that let there be *samaya* alone and not the natural relation.

Lastly, Jayanta adds that the behaviour of common man also goes in favour of *samaya* as people say in common parlance, Devadatta has said that let this meaning be understood from such and such a word'.

This is how Jayanta has dealt with the concept of relation between word and meaning. Now let us see in brief what his predecessors viz. Gautama, Vātsyāyana and Udyotakara have to say on this issue.

3.0. Gautama, Vātsyāyana and Udyotakara

Gautama has established the relation by the rule *Śabdārthavyavasthānādapratiṣedhaḥ Nyāyasūtra* 2.1.54, which means : since there is a regularity or consistency between a word and a meaning we cannot deny (the relation between the two). Vātsyāyana explains : since we understand a particular meaning from a particular word regularly we have to infer that there is a relation between them. If there is no such relation all words would denote all meanings.

(शब्दादर्थप्रत्ययस्य व्यवस्थादर्शनादनुमीयते अस्ति शब्दार्थसम्बन्धो व्यवस्थाकारणम्। असम्बन्धे हि शब्दमात्रादर्थमात्रे प्रत्ययप्रसङ्गः।

Nyāya Bhāṣya on Nyāyasūtra (2.1.54)

Udyotakara offers the form of inference : A word denotes a meaning being related to it because whatever is a cause of regular understanding reveals an object (or meaning) being related to it like a lamp—word is of such type. Therefore it also reveals the meaning being related to it.

In the next rule namely *Na, sāmayikatvāt śabdārtha-sampratyayasya. Nyāyasūtra*. 2.1.55 Gautama says that the understanding of a meaning of a word is *sāmayika* i.e. depends upon *samaya* and not on the relation.

Vātsyāyana explains : The convention that 'such and such a meaning is the connotation of such and such a word' is what is called *samaya*. When this is known a meaning is understood from a word and vice versa. Those who favour the natural relation between word and meaning also have to accept this. and knowledge of *samaya* can be had from the application of the same by the elderly persons.

To quote him:

न सम्बन्धकारितं शब्दार्थव्यवस्थानम्। किं तर्हि ? समयकारितम्। यत्तदवोचाम अस्येदमिति षष्ठीविशिष्टस्य वाक्यस्यार्थविशेषोऽनुज्ञातः शब्दार्थयोः सम्बन्ध इति, समयं तमवोचाम इति। कः पुनरयं समयः। अस्य शब्दस्य इदमर्थजातमभिधेयमिति अभिधान-अभिधेय-नियम-नियोगः। तस्मिन्नुपयुक्ते शब्दादर्थसम्प्रत्ययो भवति। विपर्यये हि शब्दश्रवणेऽपि प्रत्ययाभावः। सम्बन्धवादिनोऽपि चायमवर्जनीय इति। प्रयुज्यमानग्रहणाच्च समयोपयोगो लौकिकानाम्।

(*Nyāyabhāṣya* on *Nyāyasūtra* 2.1.55, pp. 543-44)

It will not be out of place to remember here that Kaṇāda also says *sāmayikah śabdārthapratyayah* in his *Vaiśeṣikasūtra* 7.2.20.

We can observe from this that what Jayanta is trying to defend is the stand of Vātsyāyana. He fully agrees with the Bhāṣyakāra and hence pleads for it by elaborately explaining the matter. Udyotakara, following the same stream of argument only adds: कश्चिच्च सम्बन्ध अनुज्ञातः इति यदवोचाम समयं तदवोचाम इति। (*Nyāyavārtika on Nyāya Bhāṣya on Nyāyasūtra* 2.1.55). अयं च वाच्य-वाचक-भवलक्षणः सम्बन्धः-स्वाभाविक-शब्दार्थ-सम्बन्धवादिनाऽप्यनुज्ञेयः। न हि स्वाभाविक-सम्बन्धवादिनोऽनुपयुक्तशब्दार्थसम्बन्धस्य शब्दग्रहणाद्विशेषप्रत्ययो भवति। स पुनः समयः कुतः प्रत्येतव्यः? पदज्ञानाल्लोकतश्चेति। .....मात्रादींस्तेषु तेषु अर्थेषु तांस्तान् शब्दान् प्रयुञ्जानानुपलभ्य सोऽपि तथैव शिक्षितः तांस्तानेव शब्दान् तेषु तेषु अर्थेषु प्रयुङ्क्ते न पुनरेनं लिपिमिव कश्चित् शिक्षयतीति।

(*Nyāyavārtika on Nyāya Bhāṣya on Nyāyasūtra* 2.1.55).

He has made it clear that if we say sometimes that we approve of the relation what we actually intend is nothing more than the *samaya*.

To refute the argument of the *Mīmāṁsakas* that all words are capable of expressing all meanings Gautama cites the rule *jātiviśeṣe cāniyamāt* (*Nyāyasūtra* 2.1.56) which means : there is no regularity in a particular word and a particular meaning in different people or regions, Vātsyāyana explains : Understanding of meaning from a word depends upon *samaya* and it is not natural. Because *ṛṣis, ārya* and the *mlecchas* use the words arbitrarily, for denoting certain meanings. If the relation between the two is natural then there cannot be such arbitrariness, because the cognition of colour on the basis of light does not vary from person to person. It (light) reveals the colours of things to all alike.

सामयिकः शब्दादर्थसम्प्रत्ययो न स्वाभाविकः। ऋष्यार्यम्लेच्छानां यथाकामं शब्दविनियोगोऽर्थप्रत्यायनाय प्रवर्तते। स्वाभाविके हि शब्दस्य अर्थप्रत्यायकत्वे यथाकामं न स्यात्। यथा तैजसस्य प्रकाशस्य रूपहेतुत्वं न जातिविशेषे व्यभिचरतीति।

(*Nyāya Bhāṣya on Nyāyasūtra* 2.1.56)

Udyotakara simply repeats what Vātsyāyana has stated and adds that the word *jāti* here stands for a region.

3.1. *Conclusion*

From whatever we have discussed so far the following points emerge :

(1) Jayanta is in total agreement with Gautama, Vātsyāyana and Udyotakara so far as this issue is concerned. He has as though revived their views by elaborating their arguments and by refuting systematically all the arguments of *Mīmāṁsakas* occurring in the *Śābarabhāṣya* on Jaimini 1.1.5.

(2) Gautama has used the word *samaya* in the rule 2.1.54. We shall not be able to say for the first time so confidently as Kaṇāda has also used it in his *Sūtra* 7.2.20.

(3) The word *jāti* was first used by Gautama and was taken to mean caste or different cultural levels among human beings by Vātsyāyana. Udyotakara took it in the sense of 'region' or 'province' in this particular context.
Jayanta has explained the necessity of accepting *samaya* taking both the meanings of the word *jāti* namely caste and region.

(4) The difference among meanings of a particular word as per different people or places can be explained only if *samaya* is accepted, as the convention depending upon

the desire of human being may change person to person or place to place.

In this context Jayanta reminds the *Mīmāṁsakas* that they have accepted a particular meaning as per the usage of the *mlecchas* in case of the words like *pika* or *nema* or *tāmarasa* etc. in the पिकनेमाधिकरण of Jaimini as well as the meaning of the word *rājya* as per the usage in the Andhra region in the अवेष्टयधिकरण of Jaimini. And hence, he says *samaya* is the only solution to the problem.

(5) Thus, while commenting on the *Nyāyasūtra* in his own poetic style, Jayanta, many a time has shown his independent opinions regarding various issues of philosophical importance but there are also many pleasant occasions like this one when he has agreed with the tradition in toto and as if has revived the rich system in his lucid style.

References

1. *Nyāyamañjarī* of Jayantabhaṭṭa, Ed. by S.N. Shukla, The Kashi Sanskrit Series—106, Chowkhamba Sanskrit Series Office, Varanasi, 1971.
2. *Nyāyasūtra* of Gautama, (*Nyāyadarśana*) with *Bhāṣya, Vārtika* and *Tātparyaṭīkā*, Ed. by A.M. Tarkatirtha, Munshiram Manoharlal Publishers, New Delhi, 1985.
3. *Nyāya Bhāṣya* of Vātsyāyana, As (2) above
4. *Nyāyavārtika* of Udyotakara, As (2) above
5. *Vaiśeṣikasūtras* of Kaṇāda, with Upaskāra of Śaṅkara Miśra, Ed. by S.N. Mishra, Kashi Sanskrit Series — 195 Chowkhamba Sanskrit Series Office, Varanasi, 1969.
6. *Praśastapādabhāṣya* of Praśastapāda with *Kiraṇāvalī* of Udyana, Ed. by. J.S. Jetly, Oriental Institute, Baroda, 1971.
7. *Vaiśeṣika-Upaskāra* of Śaṅkara Miśra Edition—as (5) above.
8. *Śaktivāda* of Gadādharabhaṭṭa, Ed. by Harinath Bhaṭṭācārya, Kashi Sanskrit Series — 77, Chowkhamba Sanskrit Series Office, Varanasi, 1929.
9. *Śābarabhāṣya* of Śabarasvāmin, (*Tarkapādaḥ*), Ed. by K.A. Abhyankar and G.A. Joshi, Anandashram Sanskrit Books Series — 97, Poona, 1976.
10. *Bhāṣāpariccheda* (*Kārikāvali*) of Viśvanātha Nyāyapañcānana, Ed. by Pañcānana Bhattacharya, 9, Rajakrishna Lane, Calcutta—6, 1884.

2

Is *Anuvyavasāya Laukikapratyakṣa* ?

Anuvyavasāya is *vyavasāyapratyakṣa*, i.e. the direct knowledge of *vyavasāya*. To explain : when 'x' has perceptual cognition of a pot it is produced by the contact between his eyes and the pot. When he comes to know that he has the knowledge of pot i.e. when he becomes aware of his knowledge of pot, the awareness is called *anuvyavasāya*. It is believed that *anuvyavasāya* is produced by the regular process of perception i.e. by the normal contact *saṁyukta-samavāya* between mind and the knowledge (of pot in the present case) as the knowledge resides in the soul by inherence where mind is connected by the relation of contact. (*Anuvyavasāyavādva* of Gaṅgeśa (T.C. of Gaṅgeśa, pra. kha) Ed. by Kāmākhyānāth Tarkavāgiśa, Motilal Benarsidass Delhi, Patna, Varanasi, Reprint 1974, pp. 784 to 808).

In this paper an attempt is made to investigate whether this *anuvyavasāya* is produced by the regular process of perception or it should be categorised as an extraordinary type of perception? i.e. whether it is *laukika pratyakṣa* or *alaukikapratyakṣajñāna*?

I started to think more about it when I came across the definition of *bhūtatva* given by Viśvanātha Nyāyapañcānana in his *Nyāya-Siddhānta-Muktāvali*, and his comment thereon. Let us see what exactly is the problem. Viśvanātha comments on Kārikā 26 :

पृथिव्यप्तेजोवाय्वाकाशानां भूतत्वम्। तच्च बहिरिन्द्रिय-ग्राहयविशेष-गुणवत्त्वम्। अत्र ग्राहयत्वं लौकिकप्रत्यक्षस्वरूपयोग्यत्वं बोध्यम्। तेन ज्ञातो घट इति प्रत्यक्षे ज्ञानस्याप्युपनीतभान-विषयत्वात्तद्वत्यात्मनि नातिव्याप्तिः।

Pṛthivi, ap, tejas, vāyu and *ākāśa* are the *bhūtas*. Viśvanātha has defined *bhūtatva* as *bahirindriyagrāhyaviśesaguṇavattva*, which means, *bhūtatva* is the property of possessing a *viśeṣaguṇa* (special quality) which is grasped (or known) by an external sense organ. He comments further that the word *grāhyatva* in the definition stands for *laukikapratyakṣavarūpayogyatva*. This means *grāhyatva* in this particular context is a property of being fit to be an object of an ordinary perception. Naturally, the question arises : why should *grāhyatva* be taken in this restricted sense? Viśvanātha explains: if *grāhyatva* is not taken in this restricted sense then the above definition of *bhūtatva* will over apply to *ātman*. How? Viśvanātha answers, when a person has *anuvyavasāya* of a pot i.e. when a person becomes aware of his knowledge of pot, there in that awareness knowledge is also an object and the locus of knowledge is the soul and hence over-application onto it.

To elaborate this view of Viśvanātha, Vallabhācārya in his Comm. *Kiraṇāvali* states: the awareness i.e. the *anuvyavasāya* of *ghaṭa-pratyakṣa* (perception of pot) has knowledge also as an object and it (i.e. the *anuvyavasāya*) is produced through eyes. To make it clear, basically eyes are involved in *ghaṭapratyakṣa* and hence the direct knowledge of perception of pot should also involve eyes as an instrument. This amounts to saying that be it indirectly, direct knowledge of pot is produced by eyes. Thus, knowledge, though indirectly, becomes an object of eyes, and knowledge locus of which is *ātman* is a *viśeṣaguṇa*. Thus, the definition of *bhūtatva* gets applied to *ātman* which possesses the special quality, namely, knowledge apprehended by eyes, an external sense-organ.

Eyes perceive knowledge, not only indirectly but by an extraordinary type of perception. As we know, *Naiyāyikas* have accepted three types of extraordinary contacts that produce perceptual cognition.

(1) *jñāna-lakṣaṇā-pratyāsatti* i.e., contact in the form of knowledge
(2) *sāmānyalakṣaṇā-pratyāsatti* i.e. contact in the form of generic character and
(3) *yaugika-pratyāsatti* i.e. contact of a yogin. (For details vide: *Nyāyakośa* BORI, Pune, also see: *Nyāya-Siddhāntamuktāvalī* with *Kiraṇāvalī*, Benares, 1940, pp. 209-217)

Vallabhācārya explains that the perception of knowledge by eyes mentioned above is obtained by the first kind of extraordinary contact namely *jñāna-lakṣaṇā-pratyāsatti*. In the present example, the *anuvyavasāya* acts as the contact which produces the perception. Let us see the exact nature of this contact between eyes and the knowledge of pot. It is, *cakṣuḥ-saṁyukta-manaḥ-saṁyukta ātma-samavetānuvyavasāyātmaka-ghaṭa-jñānam*. It is obvious from this expression that *anuvyavasāya* i.e. the knowledge, 'घटमहं जानामि' itself acts as the contact between eyes and *vyavasāya* and produces the *anuvyavasāya*, the knowledge of knowledge.

This is how the commentator explains why Viśvanātha has elaborated the concept of *grāhyatva* in the definition *bahirindriyagrāhyaviśeṣaguṇavattva* as discussed above.

Now the main problem is two-fold: (1) whether eyes directly or indirectly—have an access to the internal objects like knowledge etc. (2) and/or whether mind has an access to the external objects like *ghaṭa* etc. The answer to these two questions will be either in affirmative or in negative. Let us discuss about the first question first.

If the answer to it is in the affirmative then each and every case of *anuvyavasāya*, where *vyavasāya* is produced by the contact between an external sense organ and an external object should be accepted as an extraordinary type of perception where knowledge acts as the contact between the external sense-organ and the *vyavasāya* produced by its contact with an external object and it will no more remain a case of an ordinary perceptual cognition produced by mind through the contact *saṁyuktasamavāya* between mind and the knowledge namely *vyavasāyā*. Traditionally, we have been under the impression that knowledge of knowledge is produced by mind, the internal sense organ, by the contact of mind with the knowledge residing in the *atman* (*Buddhi-sukhaduḥkha-iccha-prayatnānām saṁyukta-samavāyādgrahaṇam* vide *Praśasta Pādabhāṣya*) Mind is connected with *vyavasāya* located in the *ātman* by the contact *saṁyukta-samavāya* as the mind is connected to the *āman* by contact where knowledge resides by the relation of inherence (*ātmasamavetānām saṁyuktasamavāyād grahṇam* vide *Nyāyakandali* on *Praśastapādabhāṣya*) and thus, by this contact the knowledge of knowledge comes into being, e.g. *ghaṭajñāna*. It is produced by the contact between eyes and the pot and the knowledge of *ghaṭajñāna* i.e. *anuvyavasāya* is produced by mind as explained above.

If the answer to the above question is in negative then the comment and elaboration of the concept of *grāhyatva* by *Viśvanātha* becomes redundant. Because the original expression of the definition of *bhūtatva* takes care of all external sense-organs which do not have anything to do with the internal objects.

My contention is when we say that *anuvyavasāya* is produced by mind through an ordinary contact between the mind and the *vyavasāya* namely, *saṁyukta-samavāya* we should remember two things (1) the status of the object of the *vyavasāya* and (2) the locus of that object.

Suppose, the object of *vyavasāya* is *ghaṭa*. Then as a rule it is an external object which exists outside. Thus here the question is, whether it continues to exist outside or it becomes an internal object once it is known?

If it continues to exist only externally then the involvement of external sense-organ cannot be avoided as mind has no access to external objects. But if one argues that it becomes internal by existing in knowledge by *viṣayitā* relation then in that case mind can perceive it. Then what we have been learning traditionally is quite consistent. But then in that case Viśvanātha's statement becomes superfluous.

Viśvanātha, however, is confident that his statement is over-applicable to the soul and hence he finally adds: if you are not happy with the above definition and discussion then define *bhūtatva* simply as: *ātmāvṛttiviśeṣaguṇavattvam*. (*vide Siddhāntamuktāvali* on *Karikā* 26).

In my opinion what Viśvanātha says is correct as he thinks that we cannot avoid the involvement of eyes so far as the knowledge of pot is concerned. He is right because *ghaṭa* can exist either outside or inside; it cannot exist in both the places. Once we have accepted its existence outside it becomes an external object. Now it continues to exist outside. It has no way to become an internal object. And, thus, it requires some external sense-organ for its perception. One cannot in any way avoid it. As it exists externally, even when its knowledge becomes an object of another knowledge, its status of being an external object remains intact. And so far it is intact it is the object of an external sense organ and not that of mind the internal one.

Thus, even at the stage of knowledge of knowledge of pot the involvement of eyes becomes unavoidable. And, it comes to mean that eyes are involved indirectly in the production of knowledge of knowledge—that too by the extraordinary type of contact called *jñāna-lakṣaṇā-pratyāsatti* that produces extraordinary type of perception.

Hence, *anuvyavasāya*, wherever its object i.e. *vyavasāya* has an object in the form of a thing that exists outside cannot be said to be an ordinary type of perception i.e. *laukika-pratyakṣa*, but it has to be categorised as an extraordinary type of perception i.e. a-*laukika-pratyakṣa*.

In case of *anuvyavasāya* where *vyavasāya* has an internal thing as its object, however, this problem is not there as mind has an access to all internal objects like *sukha, duḥkha* etc. Hence, *anuvyavasāya* of a *vyavasāya* having an internal thing as its object can be said to be an ordinary perception, where mind, being connected to the knowledge by the relation of *saṁyuktasamavāya* would produce the knowledge of knowledge. But so far as *anuvyavasāya* of *vuavasāya* having an external thing as its object is concerned, it has got to be categorised as an extraordinary type of perception i.e. *alaukika-pratyakṣa*.

Thus, if we conclude on the line of Viśvanātha, *anuvyavasāya* is both *laukika-pratyakṣa* and *alaukika-pratyakṣa* and not only *laukika-pratyakṣa*.

Now, let us think of the second question, that is, does mind have an access to the external objects. The answer to this question is in negative according to Viśvanātha as we have seen so far. But Vācaspati Miśra has answered this question in affirmative in his *Tātparyaṭīkā* on *Nyāyavārtika*.

He says : if mind does not have an access to the externals like pot etc. then how can the form of *anuvyavasāya* include '*ghaṭam*'. It should only say *jānāmi* and not *ghaṭam*. According to him *anuvyavasāya* is *mānasa* but its object namely *vyavasāya* requires external sense-organs because if it is not so then there will not be the categories of blind or deaf etc.

स्यादेतत्, मन एवेन्द्रियानपेक्षं बाह्ये प्रवर्तत इत्यभ्युपेयम्, अन्यथा घटमहं जानामीति ज्ञानमनिमितं स्यात्। न तावदिन्द्रियजम्, आन्तरे ज्ञाने चक्षुरादीनामप्रवृत्तेः। नाप्यनुमानादिष्वन्तर्भवति, लिङ्गाद्यभावात्। तस्मान्मानसमेवेदम्। यदि च घटादौ बाह्ये न मनः प्रवर्तते, कथं घटमिति भवेत् जानामीत्येव स्यात्। न चार्थनिरूपणमन्तरेण ज्ञानरूपनिरूपणम्, तस्माद्बाह्याभ्यन्तरविषयं मनः तथा च सर्व एव संशयो मानस इत्याशङ्क्याह भाष्यकारः-सर्वत्र प्रत्यक्षविषय इति। यद्यप्ययमीदृशोऽनुव्यवसायो मानसः तथाप्यन्धबधिरादीनामभावात्तत्पूर्वं व्यवसायोत्पत्तौ चक्षुराद्यपेक्षणीयम् अन्यथा अन्धबधिराद्यभावप्रसङ्गः। (*Vide Tātparyatīkā* of Vācaspati Miśra in the *Nyāyadarśanam* Ed. T. Tarkatirtha and A. Tarkatirtha, Munshiram Manoharlal, Delhi, pp. 122-23.)

Thus, if we accept that *anuvyavasāya* is produced by mind through *saṁyukta-samavāya* that means we are following the footsteps of Vātsyāyana and Vācaspati Miśra, but, if, we on the other hand doubt the possibility of this process of *anuvyavasāya* and we think that in the case of *anuvyavasāya* of an external object the help of external sense-organ is inevitable, that means we subscribe to the later view that *anuvyavasāya* is produced by an external sense organ (e.g. eyes) through the extra-ordinary type of perception as we have already discussed. Thus, *anuvyavasāya* according to Vācaspati Miśra and Praśastapāda is an ordinary mental perception but according to the position taken by Viśvanātha it will be of two types *laukika* and *alaukika* depending upon the two types of objects.

3

A Note on Viśvanātha's Definition of *Pratyakṣa*

0.0. Viśvanātha has defined perceptual cognition (*Pratyakṣa*) in two different ways. The first time he defines it as : *Indriyajanyam jñānam Pratyakṣam* following the definition of *Pratyakṣa* given by Gautama (in the *Nyāyasūtra* 1.1.4). He further clarifies, though all the four types of knowledges require mind—the internal sense-organ-for their production, still the knowledge, where the sense-organs themselves act as a direct instrument (*karaṇa*) in the process of its production—is called *Pratyakṣajñāna*. Here, the perceptual cognition of God is not the definitum as Gautama's *Sūtra* 1.1.4 defines the *janya-Pratyakṣa* i.e. the perceptual cognition which is a product (only).

0.1. After explaining the above definition in this way Viśvanātha has offered another definition which he says is common to both *jīvā-Pratyakṣa* and *Iśvara-Pratyakṣa*. It is this second definition of *Pratyakṣa* to which I have referred in the title of the chapter. Let us see what the definition is. It runs as follows :

अथवा ज्ञानाकरणकं ज्ञानं प्रत्यक्षम्। अनुमितौ व्याप्तिज्ञानस्योपमितौ सादृश्यज्ञानस्य शाब्दबोधे पदज्ञानस्य कारणत्वात्तत्र तत्र नातिव्याप्तिः। इदं लक्षणमीश्वरप्रत्यक्षसाधारणम्।

(Vide *Bhāṣāparicchedaḥ* with *Nyāyasiddhāntamuktāvali* with the comm. *Muktāvalisaṅgraha* by Pañcānana Bhattacharya, Satinath, Bhattacharya, 9 Rajakrishna Lane, Calcutta 6, 1884, p. 122).

Tr : "Or, (let us say like this :) knowledge where (another) knowledge does not act as an instrument (to produce it) is called perceptual cognition". Since, in Inference knowledge of invariable concomitance acts as an instrument, in Analogy knowledge of similarity, in verbal understanding knowledge of words and in remembrance an experience (i.e. knowledge produced by any of these means) acts as an instrument there is no over application of this definition to these cases of knowledge procedure. This definition is common to *Īśvara-Pratyakṣa*".

0.2. Let us concentrate on this definition of *Pratyakṣa* for this chapter, namely, *jñānākaraṇakam Jñānam Pratyakṣam*. In my opinion this sentence needs to be revised. My contention is that the compound-formation in this sentence leads to some contingency and if we form it in a different way then the contingency is over. Let us discuss in detail.

1.0. The definition in question is : *jñānākaraṇakam jñānam Pratyakṣam*. Let us decide the verbal understanding arising from this sentence. In other words, if we analyse the sentence further it will be like this : *jñānam na karaṇam yasya tajjñānam Pratyakṣam*. Because we have to dissociate the compound *jñānākaraṇakam* which will look something like *jñānam na karaṇam yasya tat* as it is a *bahuvrīhi*. Thus the sentence should mean : That knowledge is perceptual one which does not have knowledge as its instrument.

1.1. What could be the meaning of the negative particle (*nañ*) in this sentence? According to the neo-logicians a negative particle (*nañ*) has two referents namely, *saṁsargābhāva* and *anyonyābhāva*, i.e. relational absence and mutual absence. There are also criteria to decide when and where a negative particle stands for a relational absence and when and where it stands for a mutual absence. The criterion for *nañ* to stand for a mutual absence is that two nominal forms should be in the agreement of case and number to the either of which the negative particle is connected e.g. *ghaṭaḥ na paṭaḥ*—here the understanding arising from this sentence will be something like *ghaṭaḥ paṭabhinnaḥ* i.e. a pot is different from a cloth as *ghaṭaḥ* and *paṭaḥ* totally agree in case-suffix and hence the negative expresses mutual absence or difference.

1.2. In the present instance also *nañ* should stand for mutual absence as it is a similar case to the above example. Here, *karaṇam* and *jñānam* agree so far as the case-endings are concerned. Both are in nominative singular. Hence, the understanding that would arise from this sentence as per the norms of the neo-logicians will be as follows : *jñānabhinnam karaṇam yasya tajjñānam pratyakṣam.*

1.3. Another point to be remembered is, the concept of *karaṇa* by definition can be applied only in case of a *kriyā* i.e. some action which produces some result. Two definitions of *karaṇa* are well known to us : *phalāyogavyavacchinnam kāraṇam karaṇam* and *vyāpāravat asādhāraṇam kāraṇam karaṇam*. The former offered by the *prācīnanyāya* and the latter by *navyanyāya*. It is clear from these that *karaṇa* is nothing but a necessary cause in the causal complex i.e. the concept of *karaṇa* necessarily involves *kāryakāraṇabhāva* or cause and effect relationship. If both these points are considered closely and accepted then the subtle contradiction in the two sentences of Viśvanātha becomes obvious. The two sentences are: *Jñānākaraṇakam jñānam Pratyakṣam and Idam lakṣaṇam Īśvara-pratyakṣasādhāraṇam.*

1.4. As we have seen the verbal understanding of the first sentence, it means : knowledge which is produced by an instrument other than knowledge is perceptual cognition. The moment we say so Īśvara is out of picture simply because no *kārya-kāraṇabhāva* can be applied to his *jñāna* being eternal.

Thus, the definition cannot include the knowledge of *Īśvara* under its domain. It will be applicable to *jīva-Pratykṣa* only as it is produced by an instrument other than knowledge.

2.0. Now, let us look at this sentence namely, *jñānākaraṇakam jñānam pratyakṣam*, from another point of view i.e. let us attempt its verbal understanding in another possible way : it could be this : *jñānaniṣtha-karaṇatvābhāva-nirūpakam jñānam Pratykṣam.* Which means : that knowledge which describes an absence of *karaṇatva* in (another) knowledge is *pratyakṣajñāna* i.e. perceptual cognition. In other words, there is an absence of *karaṇatva in jñāna* so far as *pratyakṣajñāna* is concerned. This has two implications : (1) Either it does not say anything about the *karṇatva* so far as knowledge in the context of perceptual cognition is concerned i.e. it is just a negative statement that knowledge does not play a role of *karaṇa* in case of *Pratykṣa* or (2) it says that something other than knowledge plays the role of *karaṇa* in the production of *Pratyakṣa.*

In other words the term *karaṇatvābhāva* in the sentence stands either for relational absence or for mutual absence.

2.1. If one accepts the first statement and argues that there is no statement about *karaṇatva* that produces *Pratykṣa-jñāna* i.e. *karaṇatva* in general is denied so far as perceptual cognition is concerned (Actually we cannot do this as per the dictum : *viśeṣaniṣedhe sāmānyavidheḥ taditaraparatā* but say for argument's sake we accept it) then it would mean that *Pratyakṣajñāna* is not a *kārya* (product) because we cannot talk of its *karaṇatva*. This situation i.e. not being able to talk of *kāraṇa* can arise only if something is not *kārya* but *nitya* because there is an invariable concomitance between *karaṇatva* and *kāryatva*. And if so then the original statement will be applicable only to *Īśvarapratyakṣa* and not to *jīvapratyakṣa* which is *kārya*—and then it will not be a common definition for both.

2.2. If one accepts the second statement then obviously it is applicable to *jīvapratyakṣa* and not to the other as it is not a *kārya* and hence the contingency still stands.

3.0 Observations

If we observe carefully what we have discussed so far then the following points emerge :

(1) All the types of cognition except *nirvikalpaka pratyakṣa* require some other cognition for their production. *Nirvikalpaka Pratykṣa* is the only type where another knowledge is not involved in producing it. And no *karaṇa* (in general) is involved in *Īśvara-Pratyakṣa* as it is not a product at all.

Viśvanātha thinking that let there be a definition including both the types of direct knowledge under the domain of the same definition,tried to offer the definition we have discussed above. He must have thought that knowledges except *Pratyakṣajñāna* are *jñānakaraṇaka* i.e. having knowledge as their instrument. And the *Pratyakṣa jñāna* is not a *jñānakaraṇaka* (having knowledge as the instrument for its production). He might have applied another simple logic that if we negate 'X' it includes everything in the universe which is not 'X' *e.g.* if we say not pot or *na ghataḥ* then it will include each and everything which is not a pot. Similarly, one can form two groups namely that which has knowledge as an instrument of its production and its negative. Now, the former will include only *anumiti, upamiti* and *śābdabodha* but the latter being the negative of the former will include each and everything except the three cognitions *Anumiti, upamiti* and *śābdabodha*, i.e. it will also include the knowledge of *Īśvara*. But then what is the problem? All confusion or dispute was created by : Viśvanātha's peculiar compound formation namely : *'Jñānākaraṇakam' jñānam*. Instead of stating *ajñānakaraṇakam* he placed the negative before *karaṇaka* and it created all the controversy. Actually, what he intended to say was the same as *ajñānakaraṇaka* but he stated *jñānākaraṇaka*. (Perhaps at his time this type of compounds were in vogue). But one should be aware that what he intended to say by *jñānākaraṇaka* was actually *ajñānakaraṇaka*.

Thus the definition actually should run as : *ajñānakaraṇakam jñānam Pratyakṣam*. As I said before, *ajñānakaraṇaka* will include each and everything which is not *jñānakaraṇaka* and then the word *jñāna* in the definition will restrict it to perceptual knowledge of *jīva* and *Īśvara* without any difficulty. Then the compound should be dissolved as follows :

अज्ञानकरणकं (ज्ञानम्)
न ज्ञानकरणकं (ज्ञानम्)
ज्ञानकरणकभिन्नम् (ज्ञानम्)

But if we dissolve the compound as ज्ञानं न करणं यस्य (as most of the commentators have done), there will be an expectancy तर्हि किं करणं तस्य and that will create the difficulties already discussed before.

Hence just a change in the position of *'a'* will be sufficient to make the intention of Viśvanātha well understandable. But again if we try to peep into his mind and to investigate why he formed the compound the way he has formed it then at least one reason we find there and that is the fear he may be had in his mind that if he formed the compound the way I have suggested before i.e. the normal way of forming it his intention will be still more vague to the reader as the reader may dissolve the compound as अज्ञानं करणं यस्य that whose instrument is ignorance. This may be the case. But I still want to plead for my stand as a reader of NSM will not be a lay-man any way. Because, it will not, obviously, mean anything to a lay-man. And hence the possibility of misunderstanding Viśvanātha is very less. But certainly one cannot deny it totally.

And as a result one understands the possible reason behind the peculiar formation of the compound by Viśvanātha.

Still the confusion of the type above may arise because of that formation and hence the necessity of the above discussion.

4

Murāri Miśra on the Validity of Knowledge

The well known saying, *Murārestṛtīyaḥ panthāḥ* clearly speaks of the independence of the Third School of *Pūrvamīmāṁsā*, i.e. the school of Murāri Miśra. But unfortunately, we are not left with any clear cut outline of the doctrine of Murāri Miśra. The main reason behind this seems to be the long lost tradition of this School. The result of this is that we do not have any complete work of this great scholar available to us today. But we are not fully without hope because there is a considerable quantity of references, to his doctrine, scattered in various philosophical and logical texts, on the basis of which we can attempt to reconstruct his school of thought. For example, there are many references to Murāri in the *Prāmāṇyavāda* of Gaṅgeśopādhyāya similarly there are some references in Siddhāntamuktāvali of Viśvanātha and in many such other texts of *Nyāya* and *Mīmāṃsā* philosophy. In addition, some leaflets like *Tripādīnītinayanam, Ekādaśādyadhikaranam,* probably from the original works of Murāri, are also there to help us to get, at least some of his views on some important topics of *Pūrvamīmāṁsā*. Thus, though it is a quite stupendous task, it is very much desired that the doctrine of Murāri Miśra should be reconstructed.[1] In persuit of it a very humble attempt is made in this chapter to reconstruct Murāri's views on the validity of knowledge, which is much debated a topic in Indian philosophy.

As it is just mentioned, that the problem of the validity of knowledge is much debated a topic, all Indian philosophers do not see eye to eye on this problem. If we classify their opinions they will fall under following groups :

(i) Validity and invalidity both are internal—a view held by Sāṁkhyas.[2]

(ii) Both the validity and invalidity are external—an opinion of the *Naiyāyikas*.[3]

(iii) Invalidity is internal and validity external—a Buddhist view.[4]

(iv) Validity is internal whereas invalidity is external—the view of the *Mīmāṁsakas*.[5]

We, in this paper however, are mainly concerned with the *Mīmāṁsā* views on the validity of knowledge only. Though, this is a fact that all the three schools of *Pūrva Mīmāṁsā* unequivocally hold that knowledge is self-valid, still they differ in their explanation of this self-validity.

Before we take up the main issues for discussion, let us first make it clear what self-validity of knowledge means. Self-validity is the property of the knowledge that is self-valid. It is formally defined as the state of being an object of a cognition which is produced by the factors which reveal the cognition.[6] What does it mean? Let us try to understand this with an example.

Suppose : 'x' has perceptual knowledge of pot. Then 'x' will express this knowledge as, 'This is a pot'. In other words this will be the verbalisation of the perceptual knowledge of a pot. This knowledge is revealed by another knowledge called *anuvyavasāya* which is expressed as, 'I know a pot'. Since the *anuvyavasāya* makes 'x' aware of his knowledge of pot i.e. *vyavasāya*, this *anuvyavasāya* is called *vyavasāyagrāhaka*, the revealer of *vyavasāya* i.e. *Jñānagrāhakasāmagrī*; i.e. the factors which reveal the *vyavasāya*. In other words, this second knowledge i.e. *anuvyavasāya* has an object in the form of the first knowledge i.e. *vyavasāya*.

Thus, the factors that reveal the *vyavasāya* i.e. *jñanagrāhakasāmagrī* is *anuvyavasāya* and the object of knowledge produced by such factors (*tajjanyagrahaviṣaya*) is *vyavasāya*. Therefore, the state of being an object of a cognition which is produced by the factors which reveal the cognition (*Jñānagrāhakasāmagrījanyagrahaviṣayatva*) exists in *vyavasāya* which amounts to saying that self-validity (*svatogrāhyatva*) exists in *vyavasāya*. Therefore *vyavasāya* is self-valid.

Now, let us analyse step by step how all the three schools of *Mīmāṁsā* differ in their views while explaining this *Jñānagrāhakasāmagrī* in the above-mentioned definition of self-validity.

Let us first examine the view of *Prābhākaras*. For *Prābhākaras* knowledge is self-illumined,[7] so they do not require another knowledge to reveal one knowledge. The same knowledge reveals an object as well as itself, just like a lamp reveals all the things in a room as well as it reveals itself.[8] This also explains why *vyavasāya* itself for *Prābhākaras* is expressed as 'I know a pot', and not as, 'This is a pot'.[9] This means that *vyavasāya* has revealed not only its object i.e. *ghaṭa* but also the *vyayasāya* as well. Thus *Jñānagrāhakasāmagrī* for the *Prābhākaras* is *vyavasāya* itself, and the same *vyavasāya* i.e. *jñanagrāhakasāmagrī* produces the knowledge of validity existing in *vyavasāya*.

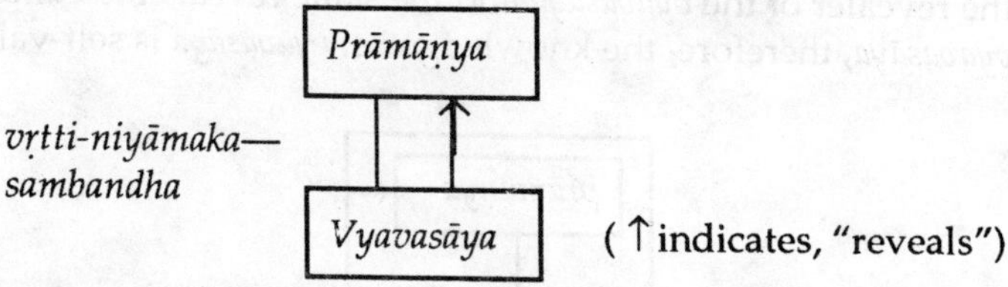

Bhāṭṭa School of *Mīmāṁsā* on the other hand holds that knowledge is supersensuous. It cannot be an object of perception. According to them knowledge is inferred on the basis of some reason (*liṅga*) which is produced in an object by knowledge. Now, what can be the probans for such an inference? They say, when an object is know by perception some property called known-ness (*jñātatā*) is produced in the same object by knowledge and on the basis of this known-ness the knowledge is inferred. The following is the form (*prayoga*) of the inference in case of the direct knowledge of a pot. The pot is the object of knowledge which possesses the potness as its qualifier and that possessed of potness as its qualificand, because it possesses known-ness qualified by potness.[10] On the basis of this inference of knowledge based on known-ness, the validity existing in the same knowledge is known.

Thus, according to the Bhāṭṭas this inferential knowledge reveals the validity existing in the *vyavasāya*, therefore, this inference is the *sāmagri* which reveals the knowledge i.e. *vyavasāya* and the knowledge produced by such inference i.e. inferential knowledge only produces the knowledge of validity existing in *vyavasāya*. In this way, *vyavasāya* is self-valid for the *Bhāṭṭas*.[11]

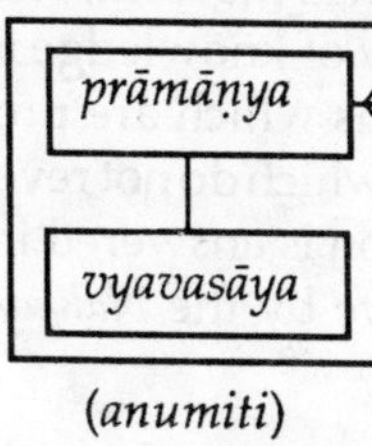

(*anumiti*)

Now we proceed to the Third school of *Pūrvamīmaṁsā* i.e. the school of Murāri Miśra. According to Murāri Miśra however *anuvyavasāya* reveals the validity of *vyavasāya*. For him also, the form of *vyavasāya* in case of the direct knowledge of a Pot is, 'This is a pot'. And the second knowledge i.e. the awareness about the first knowledge i.e. *anuvyavasāya* is 'I know a pot'.

As this *anuvyavasāya* reveals *vyavasāya* it also reveals the validity existing in *vyavasāya* Murāri holds. Thus, *anuvyavasāya* is the revealer of the *vyavasāya* and the same reveals the validity in *vyavasāya*, therefore, the knowledge i.e. *vyavasāya* is self-valid.[12]

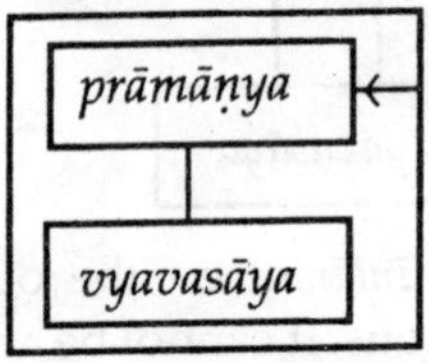

(*anuvyavasāya*)

Thus, as far as the self-validity of knowledge i.e. the state of being an object of a cognition which is produced by the factors which reveal the cognition, is concerned all the three schools of *Mīmāṁsā* agree to it but they differ in stating what the *sāmagri* is.

As we have seen above, according to the *Prābhākaras* this *sāmagrī* is *vyavasāya* itself, according to the *Bhāṭṭas* this *sāmagrī* is *anumiti* and according to the school of Murāri Miśra this *sāmagri* is *anuvyavasāya*.

Now let us turn to the *prāmāṇyāvāda* of *Taṭtvacintāmaṇi* where Gaṅgeśopadhāyaya has discussed five forms of the self-validity of knowledge. We have chosen here, only the first form for discussion out of the five.

The first form runs as follows : ज्ञानप्रामाण्यं तद-प्रामाण्याग्राहक-यावज्ज्ञानग्राहकसामग्रीग्राह्यं न वा[13] Let us look into the meaning of this form first and then we shall discuss the propriety of each and every expression in the form, one by one. The meaning : whether or not the validity of knowledge is the state of being an object of all those cognitions which are produced by the factors which reveal cognition and which do not reveal the invalidity of the same cognition. The question is answered in affirmative by the— *Mīmāṁsakas* and in negative by the *Naiyāyikas*. In other words, affirmative answer to the question leads to the theory of self-validity of knowledge and vis-a-vis.

We have just seen the meaning of the expression *jñānagrāhakasāmagrī*. We have also observed that there are three qualifiers of this *sāmagrī* in the above mentioned first form of self-validity of knowledge discussed by Gaṅgeśopādhāya. Let us now discuss the propriety and purpose of adding these qualifiers.

First of all we shall discuss the necessity of adding *yāvat* as an adjective to *sāmagrī*. *Yavāt* means as many, so many i.e. all. Although it appears—apparently to be an adjective of *sāmagrī* as it is impossible because the diverse factors cannot produce a single knowledge,[14] it requires to be interpreted as a qualifier of *graha* (knowledge) because otherwise there will arise the contingency of having no contradiction with the theory of *Naiyāyikus*. No such contingency will arise however if it qualifies the knowledge. How? Let us discuss in details in order to catch the point.

According to the *Naiyāyikas* the validity of knowledge is known by an inference like, 'This knowledge is valid, since it has produced fruitful inducement.[15] Now if the word *yāvat* is totally dropped, the definition will get applied to any knowledge which includes inferential knowledge as well, and in that case there will arise a contingency called *siddhasādhanatva*.[16] If the *Mīmāṁsakas* also accept that inferential cognition reveals the validity of knowledge then there is no need of raising such a question as, whether a knowledge is self-valid. Thus, to avoid all this the word *yāvat* is added.

With this addition the form under discussion will mean : Whether or not, the validity of knowledge is known by all possible and accepted knowledges namely, *vyavasāya*, *anuvyavasāya* etc. produced by the factors that reveal the knowledge but do not reveal the non-validity of the knowledge. Thus, by adding *yāvat* the cognitions like *vyavasāya* etc. are included, with which the *Naiyāyikas* will not agree. Because, the *Naiyāyikas* accept that *anumiti* alone reveals the validity of knowledge and never a *vyavasāya* or an *anuvyavasāya*.[17] In this way, the word *yāvat* establishes the contradiction.

Now, let us examine the propriety of the qualifier *aprāmāṇyāgrāhaka* i.e. that which does not reveal the invalidity. Suppose, this adjective of *sāmagrī* is absent then what would be the result? Obviously, there will arise a contingency that an invalid knowledge also will be called self-valied, what does it mean? Let us consider one case where such a contingency may arise : Let us take up the case of knowledge, 'This knowledge is false'. That this knowledge is false is a fact. Now, if the condition *aprāmāṇyāgrāhaka* is not laid down, the invalidity existing in the above knowledge will not be revealed and as a consequence of this, the above-mentioned knowledge will have to be treated as valid. Thus in order to exclude such an incorrect knowledge from the expression this adjective is added.

Moreover; only that which does not reveal the invalidity is not a sufficient condition but one should add which does not reveal the invalidity of the same knowledge, i.e. *vyavasāya*. Why? In the above-said example, i.e. 'This knowledge is false', the *anuvyavasāya* of it is a valid cognition, but nevertheless it reveals the invalidity of *vyavasāya*. Here, *vyavasāya* will become self-valid, which in fact is invalid unless we specify the locus of the validity to be revealed, and that of the invalidity not to be revealed. This is achieved by adding the adjective '*tadaprāmāṇyāgrahakā*' in the statement.

Thus, the self-validity means not requiring any factor, other than those required for the revelation; of the knowledge, and the validity existing therein. Having understood in this way, the exact implication of the theory of self-validity let us now construct the theories of self-validity relating to all the three schools of Mīmāṁsā, and then let us attempt to show how the same statement is true and uniformly applicable to all these three schools.

Self-validity accordingly to the Prābhākara school : Let us take one example, in order to construct the whole theory of this school. Suppose 'x' has a direct knowledge of a pot. This knowledge is produced, say, by the contact of the sense-organs and the object. Since, according to the school of Prābhākara, knowledge is self-illumined, the form of the *vyavasāya* will be, 'I know the pot'. Now, as 'x' has the knowledge of a pot, as per the statement of self-validity the knowledge is revealed by the same knowledge and the factors which revealed the knowledge also revealed the validity of the knowledge. Now, what are the factors here which revealed the knowledge? Naturally, according to Prābhākara it is *vyavasāya* only.[18]

Thus the validity existing in *vyavasāya* is known by the factors which revealed *vyavasāya* namely the *vyavasāya* itself. So the knowledge i.e. *vyavasāya* is self-valid. Again since the same *vyavasāya* did not reveal the invalidity existing in itself it is self-valid according to the definition of self-validity.

For the Bhāṭṭa school of *Mīmāṁsā* the process is not so simple, because as we know knowledge is inferred according to them and not perceived as knowledge is beyond the reach of any sense-organs (*atīndriya*). So when 'x' has a knowledge of an object say, pot, that is when the *vyavasāya* is there as, 'This is a pot' some property called knownness (*jñātatā*) is produced in the pot and on the basis of this knownness as probans the knowledge is inferred. The following is the form and process of the inference : The pot forms the object of the knowledge which has the pot as its qualificand and the potness as its qualifier. Because it possesses the property called knownness qualified by potness.[19] On the basis of such inference the knowledge is inferred.

Here, the factors which produced this inferential cognition are *parāmarśa* etc. as they produce this inferential cognition which reveals the validity of the knowledge i.e. of *vyavasāya*. Thus, as per the generalisation expressed in the statement *vyavasāya* is self-valid for the Bhāṭṭas also.

Now let us see the position of the third school of *Pūrvamīmāṁsā*. Murāri Miśra i.e. the exponent of the third school holds that *anuvyavasāya* reveals the validity existing in *vyavasāya*. Thus for this school, the form of the *vyavasāya* is, 'This is a pot', and the form of the *anuvyavasāya* is, 'I know a pot' and the same i.e. *anuvyavasāya* reveals the validity of *vyavasāya*.

According to Murāri the fact is as follows. The second knowledge is the direct knowledge or after knowledge of the first knowledge. In other words, an *anuvyavasāya* has *vyavasāya* as its object, which is produced by the contact of sense-organs and an object. An *anuvyavasāya* is produced by mind. Nevertheless it is a perceptual knowledge. The following is the process of its production : By definition any perceptual knowledge has to be produced by sense-organ and object-contact.[21] What could be the contact here? The object here is the knowledge *vyavasāya*, which is the quality of the soul. Since the object is internal no external sense-organ can come in contact with this knowledge which is internal. Naturally the sense-organ will be the mind itself. What is the contact? The contact is obviously *saṁyukta-samavāya*, because the mind is connected with the soul by the relation of contact. In the soul the knowledge is present by the relation of inherence. Thus, the contact between the mind and the object namely the *vyavasāya* will be *saṁyukta-samavāya*. This contact is one of the factors which produce the direct knowledge of *vyavasāya* i.e. *anuvyavasāya*.[22] And this *anuvyavasāya* reveals the validity of the *vyavasāya*. In this way, a *vyavasāya* is self-valid for the Miśra-school.

The above description of the theories of self-validity also clearly demonstrates how the statement of self-validity is uniformly applicable to all the three schools of *Pūrvamīmāṁsā*. This could be possible because of the word, *yāvat*, introduced in the statement which incorporates all possible opinions of the *Mīmāṁsakas*. Thus *vyavasāya, anumiti* and *anuvyavasāya* are included as the revealers of this validity with which the *Naiyāyikas* disagree.

Some remarks on the stand of Murāri Miśra regarding the theory of self-validity are in order. The above discussion has amply demonstrated the fact that it is this view of Murāri on the validity of knowledge which has been time and again quoted since the time of Gaṅgeśa upto recent commentators. Thus, it is not unlikely that Murāri was recognised as the holder of the new school of thought because of his this very doctrine. His other views might have been treated as marginal ones. It seems that Murāri is very much influenced by the Nyāya school in this context. Though he maintains that knowledge is self-valid like the other two schools of *Mīmāṁsā*, he accepts many concept of the *Naiyāyikas*. For example : he accepts that the object of *anuvyavasāya* is *vyavasāya*. By accepting this he distinguishes his doctrine from that of *Prābhākaras* and *Bhāṭṭas*. Nevertheless he accepts that **अनुव्यवसाय** is **व्यवसायप्रत्यक्ष** which amounts to saying that knowledge is known by perception, which is a Nyāya view.

He accepts *manas* as an internal sense-organs for the perception of internal object.[23] This is also basically a *Nyāya* concept.

Notes and References

1. Vide Dr. Umeśa Mishra, *Murārestṛtiyaḥ panthāḥ*, Proceedings and Transactions of the Fifth Indian Oriental Conference, volume II, 1930, p. 967.
2. *Śāstradipikā*, Chowkhambā Sanskrit Series, NO. 188, p. 54.
3. Ibid, p. 54.
4. Ibid, p. 54.
5. Ibid, p. 54.
6. Comm. on *Tarkadipikā*, The Kashi Sanskrit Series, No. 187, p. 358.

7. *Prakaraṇa Pañcikā*, Banaras Hindu University Darsana Series, No. 4, p. 172. (ii) ibid, p. 173.
8. Ibid, p. 172.
9. *Rāmarudriyam* on *Tarkadīpikā*, Kashi Sanskrit Series, 187, p. 359.
10. *Nīlakaṇṭhaprakāśikā* on *Tarkadīpikā*, p. 360.
11. *Ślokavārtika*, Madras University Sanskrit Series, , p. 48.
12. *Rahasya* on *Tattvacintāmaṇi*, Bibliotheca Indica : A collection of Oriental work, p. 126.
13. Vide *Tattvacintāmaṇi*, pp. 121-122.
14. *Nīlakaṇṭhaprakāśikā* on Tarkadipikā, pp. 360-61.
15. *Nṛsimhaprakāśikā* on *Tarkadīpikā*.
16. *Tarkadīpikā*,
17. *Siddhāntamuktāvalī*, Kashi Sanskrit Series, No. 212, p. 438.
18. *Rāmarudrīyam* on *Tarkadīpikā*, p. 359.
19. Vide foot-note 10, above.
20. *Rāmarudrīyam* on *Tarkadīpikā*, p.360.
21. *Nyāyasūtra*, Chowkhambā Sanskrit Series, p. 58.
22. *Rāmarudrīyam* on *Tarkadīpikā*, p.360. Also look into the second chapter of this book for more discussion on *anuvyavasāya*.
23. Vardhamana's *Prakāśa* on *Kusumāñjaliprakaraṇa*, p. 219. Quoted by Umeśa Miśra. Proceeding. Fifth Indian Oriental Conference, II, p. 986.

5

On Qualifier and Indicator

The name of Murāri Miśra, the exponent of the third school of *Pūrvamīmāṁsā* is not so unfamiliar in the world of Sanskritists. It is because of the well known saying. *'Murāres tṛtiyaḥ panthāḥ'* and also because of the references to his name and to his distinct views on various topics occurring in various philosophical texts.[1] But it is a fact that his views on various important topics in Indian philosophy are not so well known for certain reasons into which we need not enter here. One of such important topics in Indian philosophy is that of *viśeṣaṇa* and *upalakṣaṇa*. In this chapter I propose to discuss the concepts of *Viśeṣaṇa* and *upalakṣaṇa* as per the definitions given by Murāri Miśra in one of his works namely, *'Tripādīnītinayaṇam'*.[2] Before we take up the definitions given by *Murāri* for discussion, let us see how the other systems of Indian Philosophy conceive these two terms namely, *viśeṣaṇa* and *upalakṣaṇa*. Accordingly, the paper is divided into four parts :

(i) *Mīmāṁsaka's* Option
(ii) *Naiyāyikas'* Standpoint
(iii) Murāri's Conception
(iv) Conclusion

Although we are mainly concerned in this paper to discuss, compare and contrast the concepts of *Viśeṣaṇa* and *upalakṣaṇa* of Murāri in the background of Bhāṭṭa school of *Mīmāṁsā*, Prābhākara school of *Mīmāṁsā* and *Nyāya* system of Indian philosophy, still a line or two about the position of these concepts in Pāṇini, Kātyāyana and Patañjali will not be out of the place.

Pāṇini uses the word *Viśeṣaṇa* in the rule 2.1.57 i.e. *Viśeṣaṇam Viśeṣyeṇa bahulam* and in 1.2.52 i.e. *Viśeṣaṇānām cājāteḥ*, and the word *lakṣaṇa* in the rule (2.3.21, i.e.) *itthambhūtalakṣaṇe*. In the rule 2.1.57 he states a pair of concepts. The word *Viśeṣaṇa* is paraphrased as *Viśeṣaka* by *Kātyāyana* and as *bhedaka* by *Kāśikākāra*. *Kāśikākāra* also paraphrases *viśeṣya* as *bhedya*. Thus, what distinguishes is a *Viśeṣaṇa*. Udyota makes it further specific by rendering the pair as *Vyāvartya* and *Vyāvartaka*. Needless to say that this paraphrasing is based on later development in systems like *Mīmāṁsā* and *Nyāya*.

(I) Mīmāṁsakas' Opinion

Although any elaborated discussion on the conceptual analysis is not found in any mīmāṁsā texts still from the use of these terms in those texts and from the contexts in which these are used, we can form some ideas about *Mīmāṁsakas'* concepts of *viśeṣaṇa* and *upalakṣaṇa*.

While pleading for his own doctrine of *ākṛti* as the expressed sense of a word Śabara states that if a *viśeṣaṇa* is not known to a person, he cannot have *Viśiṣṭa-jñāna*.[3] Thus, since it is observed that after hearing the word go one gets the knowledge of *gotva-viśiṣṭa-go* which is a *Viśiṣṭa-jñāna*, it is necessary that one must have the knowledge of *gotva* prior to the knowledge of *gotva-viśiṣṭa-go*.

Naturally, if the word *go* is to generate a *Viśiṣṭajñāna, gotva* must be known from the word itself. Therefore, it is argued that the word *go* expressed *gotva* i.e. *ākṛti* and the individual i.e. *gotva-viśiṣṭa-go* is understood by implication.

The opponent holds that an individual indicated by an *ākṛti* is the expressed sense of a word. To refute this position of the opponent, Śabara argues, let us compare two words *daṇḍin* and *go*. Both these words generate *Viśiṣṭa-jñāna*. We have already noted that the word *go* generates the knowledge of *gotva-viśiṣṭa-go*. Similarly, the word *daṇḍin* also generates the knowledge of a man with a stick which also is a *Viśiṣṭa-jñāna*. But in the knowledge of 'a man with a stick' we can account for the knowledge of stick from the part of the same word *i.e.* from *daṇḍa* and man from the suffix *in*. Whereas there is no part in the word go which can be taken to express *gotva*. Naturally, as the *viśeṣaṇa* cannot be understood from any part of this word and since without the knowledge of it, the qualified knowledge is impossible to occur, it should be accepted that the word go itself express *gotva*.[4]

Śabara does not use the word *upalakṣaṇa* but he uses two words, namely *lakṣaṇa* and *cihna* in the sense of *Upalakṣaṇa*. He has not defined *Viśeṣaṇa* but in the same context, the opponent argues, let *gotva* be *lakṣaṇa* or mark for the individual, which belongs to the class of '*go*'. And if it is the case then the knowledge of *Vyakti* will be qualified knowledge. If it is a qualified knowledge then the *Viśeṣaṇa* should be known earlier, because, if *Viśeṣaṇa* is not known *Viśiṣṭa-jñāna* cannot arise. Therefore, let the word express the *ākṛti* as *Viśeṣaṇa* and *Vyakti* as *Viśeṣya*.

Needless to say that this view is not acceptable to Śabara. he argues, unless *Viśeṣaṇajñāna* is there, *Viśiṣṭajñāna* cannot arise i.e. in other words *Viśeṣaṇajñāna* is the cause of *Viśiṣṭajñāna*, Therefore, let *Viśeṣaṇa* i.e. *ākṛti* be expressed by the word, and *Viśeṣya* will be known by implication.

It is very clear from this discussion that Śabara talks of these two terms i.e. *Viśeṣaṇa* and *Upalakṣaṇa* in the context of a qualified knowledge. Naturally, according to him, both these terms are expressive of *Prakāra* or qualifier in a qualified cognition.

Kumārila expressed his views on this issue in his *Tantravārtika* which are in full agreement with Śabara's Bhāṣya. Kumārila clearly states that *Viśeṣaṇa* as well as *upalakṣaṇa* are the distinguishers or qualifiers.[5]

While explaining the comparison between the two words i.e. *daṇḍin* and *go*, offered by Śabara, Kumārila adds one more example of *upalakṣaṇa*. He says that, it is not improper to hold that the *Viśeṣya* is conveyed by a word like *daṇḍin* or *devadattagṛha* because the *Viśeṣaṇa* i.e. *Prakāra* namely, the *daṇḍa* and *kākanilayana* can be known by word and by perception respectively in the case of *daṇḍī puruṣah* and *kākavad devadatta-gṛham*. But such is not the case with the word *go*. Because there is no part in it which can generate the cognition of *gotva*.[6] And unless *gotva* i.e. *Viśeṣaṇa* is known there cannot arise a qualified knowledge from the word *go*. Thus, Kumārila says that since *viśiṣṭa-jñāna* occurs when we hear the word *go*, it means that *Viśeṣaṇa* is known, and since it is not known from any other means as mentioned above, *gotva* itself is to be treated as the *Vācya* i.e. expressed meaning of the word *go* and the individual is understood by implication.

It is interesting to note that Kumārila replaced the word *lakṣaṇa*, used by Śabara, by *upalakṣaṇa*, in the same sense of *china* as used by Śabara. Nevertheless it is different from *Viśeṣaṇa*.

Now let us turn to the Prābhākara school of *Pūrvamīmāṁsā*. In the *Bṛhatī* of Prabhākara Miśra we get still better picture because Prabhākara discusses the issue a bit more elaborately, in the same context i.e. *ākṛti* is the expressed meaning of a word.

Prabhākara in a way tries to define *upalakṣaṇa* which was not done either by *Śabara* or by Kumārila. He states : *upalakṣaṇam hi nāma nātmākāratayā upalakṣyam upalkṣyayati*[7] and gives an example : *'Yathā yatra ayam kākaḥ ado devadattasya gṛham iti na kākākāram gṛaham avasīyate.*[8] That is, *Upalakṣaṇa* say 'x', is that which does not indicate something say 'y' in the form of 'x'. For instance, the house of Devadatta is not presented in the knowledge as identical with the crow by the expression, *'Yatra ayam kākaḥ ado devadattasya gṛham'*. In other words, *Kāka* i.e. crow does not generate an understanding of the house as crow, but as distinct from crow.

Prabhākara makes his idea of *upalakṣaṇa* further clear by giving another example. The examples is of *pañjsarastha simha,*[9] i.e. a lion in a cage and it is explained by *Śālikanātha* in Ṛjuvimalā as, suppose, one has seen a lion always in a cage, it is but natural that whenever he hears the word *Simha* he understands a *pañjara* as well. Similarly, when *Vyakti* is understood from the word *go, gotva* is regularly understood along with it because of the regular association.[10] Thus, individual can be the expressed meaning of a word and the *ākṛti* could be understood by indication. This is the stand of the opponent which is answered by Prabhākara in following way : he says that, it is true that such a person understands the cage also, whenever he hears the word lion, but he understands it as being different from the lion. That is to say, he does not understand the cage in the form of lion but as distinct from the lion. It is not true in the case of *go* and *gotva*. That is, the cowness is not understood as different from cow. Thus, the example given by the opponent does not prove the contrary.[11]

Needless to say that we are not concerned with the argument about the meaning of the word here, but, nevertheless this discussion helps us form the idea of *upalakṣaṇa* in the mind of Prabhākara.

The concept of *upalakṣaṇa* is further elaborated by Prabhākara as follows : *Yatra ākārāntaravivekaḥ tatra ākārāntaram upalakṣaṇam. Yathā daṇḍī ityeva dandī-viśeṣa-avagatau na ānayane daṇḍasya anvayaḥ. Yatra punaḥ daṇḍītayā eva avagamyate na viśeṣataḥ tatra tathābhūtasyaiva anvayaḥ śakyate vaktum.*[12]

That is, when something, say 'x' is known distinct from something say 'y' 'x' is called *upalakṣaṇa*. For instance, when the very word *daṇḍī* is expressed to indicate some particular person, the stick is nothing but a mark which indicates that person. And in that case in the expression '*daṇḍinam ānaya*' the stick need not be connected with the act of bringing. But when some particular person is not conveyed by the word *daṇḍin* but 'a person with a stick then naturally the stick is a *Viśeṣaṇa* and it is not an *upalakṣaṇa* or indicator any more, and in such a case, the stick is connected with *kārya* i.e. an action say, bringing. This clearly reveals the view of Prabhākara that *upalakṣaṇa* is not connected with an action. Moreover, he has expressed this view himself when he says '*upalakṣaṇatve na aṇgam bhavati*.[13]

It can be observed from this that Prābhākara also does not talk of *viśeṣaṇa* so elaborately. He only states keeping in line with the *Śabarabhāsya* that the knowledge of *viśeṣaṇa* before *Viśiṣṭa-jñāna* is essential.[14] Nevertheless it is clear that it is Prabhākara who attempted to define the concept of *upalakṣaṇa*, for the first time. In other words, he provided a criterion to decide whether 'x' is *upalakṣaṇa* or not, over and above that 'x' is a mark.

Bhavanātha, a follower of the Prābhākara school puts the same concept in the *Mīmāṁsānayaviveka*[15] as '*pṛthag bhūte hi dharmiṇy upalakṣaṇam*.[16]

That is, when something known is different from that on the basis of which it is known then that on the basis of which it is known is called *upalakṣaṇa*. This is how this definition is explained by the commentator Varadarāja : To be more precise, When something, say, 'x' is known as differentiated on account of something say, 'y' then 'y' is called *upalakṣaṇa*.[17] Thus, the house of Devadatta is known as differentiated on account of *kāka* but of course, as a house of Devadatta only then *kāka* is an *upalakṣaṇa*. But this is not the case with *Viśeṣaṇa* obviously because, it is not the case that cow, possessed of cowness is known on account of some property other than cowness. Naturally, cowness is a *Viśeṣaṇa* and so the expressed meaning of the word *go* has to be *gotva*. Bhavanātha establishes this point with the same example given by *Prābhākara*.[18]

From the above discussion by both the schools of *Mīmāṁsā* we obverse that there is full agreement with the fact that cowness, in the knowledge of cow with cowness, arising from the word *go* is a qualifier and cannot be treated as an indicator, whereas the crow, in the knowledge of Devadatta's house arising on account of crow, is nothing but an indicator. The only contribution if claimed by Prābhākara is a positive attempt to define the concept of *upalakṣaṇa*.

Although they have not talked much about *viśeṣaṇa*, excepting the *Bhāṣya* statement that, that which is directly connected is *viśeṣaṇa* and that which is distantly connected cannot produce a qualified knowledge, by implication, they treat *viśeṣaṇa* as something which is directly connected to the *Viśeṣya* in the knowledge.

(II) Naiyāyikas Standpoint

Let us now turn to the *Naiyāyikas*. Unlike the *Bhāṭṭas* they concentrated on defining these two concepts right from the beginning. if was Udayana among the old *Naiyāyikas*, who in his *Kiranāvali*, initiated a scientific definition of these terms.[19] The discussion occurs in the context of a qualified knowledge, *'dve dravye'* i.e. 'there are two substances'. In this cognition number two, i.e. *dvitva* is *viśeṣaṇa* and the substances are the *viśeṣya*. But the problem is, according to the metaphysical and ontological stand of the *Nyāyavaiśeṣika* system, number two onwards all higher numbers are produced by a knowledge called *apekṣā-buddhi* and since knowledge is not a permanent entity, after disappearance of the *apekṣā-buddhi* the number two is bound to disappear. In the process of congition, by the time one gets the qualified cognition, (there are) two substances, number two has already disappeared.[20]

Naturally, the question arises: how does this knowledge take place because *dvitva* i.e. *viśeṣaṇa* is not present at time of this knowledge. In a reply to this question, Udayana argues that although *viśeṣaṇa* or qualifier is the cause of the *Viśiṣṭa-jñāna* or qualified knowledge, it need not be an object of the same knowledge.[21] Therefore, though *dvitva* i.e. number two is not present at the time of the *Viśiṣṭa-jñāna*, the knowledge of it can be the cause of the qualified knowledge *'dve dravye'* and thereby its state of being a *viśeṣaṇa* remains intact.[22] The only condition for being *viśeṣaṇa* is that, it must exist in the same *Viśeṣya* which is the *viśeṣya* of the qualified knowledge.

Thus, Udayana defines *viśeṣaṇa* as, *samānādhikaraṇam avacchedakam viśeṣaṇam*[23] i.e. a *viśeṣaṇa* is that, which distinguishes its locus being existent in the same locus. He also illustrates the case with the example of *nīlam utpalam*.[24] Here, the blue colour, being present in it distinguishes the locus of the blue colour, from the loci of red, white etc. Therefore, blue colour is a qualifier.

He defines *upalakṣaṇa* as *'avacchedakatva aviśeṣe' pi vyadhikaraṇam upalakṣaṇam.*[25] It means : an *upalakṣaṇa* is that which distinguishes a locus which is not its locus. No example of *upalakṣaṇa* is given by Udayana. But it is quite obvious from the definition that when the *kāka* is not connected with the house of Devadatta, at the same time it distinguishes the house, it is *upalakṣaṇa*.

It is quite apparent from the definition offered by Udayana, that both the *viśeṣaṇa* and *upalakṣaṇa* share the nature of differentiating something from the other, which is in quite accordance with Kumārila. In addition, Udayana has also provided the criterion to distinguish *viśeṣaṇa* from *upalakṣaṇa* namely, *samānādhikaraṇatva* and *vyadhikaraṇatva*.

In his *Saptapadārthi*, Śivāditya Miśra reproduces Udayana's definitions of *viśeṣaṇa* and *upalakṣaṇa* by simply replacing the word *avacchedaka* by *vyāyartaka*. Thus, the respective definitions are : *Samānādhikaraṇam vyāvartakam viśeṣaṇam* and *Vyadhikaraṇam sad Vyāvartakam upalakṣaṇam.*[26]

It is worth noticing that he gives his own interpretation of the word *sāmanādhikaraṇya* and *Vaiyadhikaraṇya.*[27] He interprets *Sāmanādhikaraṇya* as *ekevibhaktyantapadavācyatvam*[28] and *vaiyadhikaraṇya* as *bhinnavibhaktyantapadavācyatvam.*[29]

Thus, Śivāditya tries to define these concepts formally. If there is a formal agreement of adjectival and substantive forms, it is *viśeṣaṇa* whereas, if there is no such agreement it is a case of *upalakṣaṇa*. Naturally, in *rūpavān ghaṭaḥ, rupa* is *viśeṣaṇa*, whereas in case of *jaṭābhiḥ tāpasaḥ, jaṭā* is *upalakṣaṇa.*[30]

When we come to Gaṅgeśa, we find that an elaborate discussion (*vāda*) is added by him in his *Tattvacintāmaṇi* where he has taken into account various previous definitions given by his predecessors.

While refuting Śivāditya's interpretation of *sāmānādhikaraṇya* Gaṅgeśa argues that if *viśeṣaṇatva* is defined as *'viśeṣyasamānavibhaktikatvam'* the definition will over apply to the case of *Kākavaddevadattagṛham*, where *kāka*, in fact is *upalakṣaṇa* and not *viśeṣaṇa.*[31]

The commentator Rucidatta adds that it will not only apply to the crow but also to the string of the expression *ghaṭaḥ paṭaḥ* etc. because here too both *ghaṭa* and *paṭa* show one and the same nominative ending.[32]

In this way, having refuted some other views Gaṅgeśa gives his own view. He explains the point as follows : After the qualified knowledge namely, *daṇḍī puruṣaḥ* i.e. 'a person with a stick', has occurred, it is understood that the 'person with a stick' is different from those who do not have sticks. Although there are two properties in the person namely, *daṇḍa* and *puruṣatva*, the locusness of difference in the person with the stick is delimited by the stick and not by *Puruṣatva* (personness), because in that case *puruṣatva* cannot differentiate this person from other persons who do not have sticks simply because in them too *puruṣatva* exists. Not only that, even at the time when the stick is not with that person there is no difference of that person from other persons (who do not have sticks) and as such no difference exists in that person and so no knowledge of difference is possible. Therefore, *daṇḍa* alone is the delimitor of the locusness of difference in the 'person with the stick'.[33]

In case of *kākavad devadatta-gṛham*, of course, the difference from all those houses that are not of Devadatta is understood in the house of Devadatta but the delimitor of this locusness of the difference cannot be *kāka* since even in the absence of *kāka* namely when *kāka* is moving in circle over the house of Devadatta or when it was associated with the house in the past, the difference is known alike.[34]

The following is the main difference between these two concepts according to Gaṅgeśa :

The knowledge of difference in the qualified object cannot occur in the absence of *Viśeṣaṇa*, whereas, even if the *upalakṣaṇa* is absent it can cause the knowledge of difference through its own knowledge.

Accordingly, Gaṅgeśa defines *viśeṣaṇa* and *upalakṣaṇa* as follows :

That which distinguished something from other being a delimitor of the locusness of the difference to be known is a *Viśeṣaṇa* and any other distinguisher different from it is called *upalakṣaṇa*.

Gadādhara, while explaining the rule of Pāṇini *itthambhūtalaksaṇe'* (p. 2.3.21), looks at this problem in a bit different way.[36]

He has tried to establish that *viśeṣaṇa* is understood from a possessive suffix, whereas, *upalakṣaṇa* is known by an Instrumental suffix.[37] For example, *daṇḍī puruṣaḥ* and *jaṭābhiḥ tāpasaḥ*. Here *daṇḍa* is *viśeṣaṇa* because it is understood from, a word ending in the possessive suffix—*in*, whereas, *jaṭā* is *upalakṣaṇa* because it is understood from a word ending in Instrumental.[38]

If this view is accepted then both *kāka* and *jaṭā* will have to be treated as *viśeṣaṇa* in the expressions, *kakavad devadatta gṛham* and *jaṭāvān tāpasaḥ*, which is contrary to the fact as it is shown by Gaṅgeśa.

No doubt it would have been an ideal position to corelate one particular concept with one particular expression, but it cannot be maintained since in the expression, *kākavad devadattasya gṛham*, *'kāka'* is treated by all as *upalakṣaṇa*.

Śaṅkara Miśra on the other hand, makes a very bold statement in his *Upaskāra* as follows :

Yadā Devadattagṛhe kākavattā tadā kākah viśeṣaṇam eva, Yadā tu upari bhraman asan kākaḥ tadā upalakṣaṇam[39]

Thus, according to this view, when crow sits on the house of Devadatta it is *viśeṣaṇa* and the same crow if it is not connected with the house but if on the basis of its knowledge Devadatta's house is known it can be called *upalakṣaṇa*.

What is deduced form Śaṅkra Miśra is, when a person observes the crow sitting on the house, the crow must be treated as *viśeṣaṇa* because in the knowledge the crow itself appears as a qualifier of the house, but when the crow is not there and still one gets the knowledge of the house on account of the previous existence of the crow on the house, the crow does not appear as the qualifier of the house, but mere structure of the house indicated by the knowledge of the crow appears as the qualifier of the house and so crow is called *upalakṣaṇa*.

This is how the *Naiyāyikas* have contributed to these notions by way of defining these concepts as comprehensively as possible in order to include all cases, discussed above.

(III) Murāri's View

Coming to Murāri we find that in his *Tripādīnīthinayana* he has offered a different set of the definitions of *Viśeṣaṇa* and *upalakṣaṇa*. The context in which Murāri defines these two terms is the question of establishing a connection between the *arthavāda* sentences and the *vidhi* sentences i.e. between the *prāśastya* and the *vidheya* i.e. *Yāga*. Murāri holds that *Prāśastya* i.e. praise (of deity i.e. the constituent of the sacrifice) is an *upalakṣaṇa* to *yāga* i.e. sacrifice[40] and then defines the two terms i.e. *viśeṣaṇa* and *upalakṣaṇa* as intended by him.

When he starts defining, the beginning remark itself is surprising. He says : *Na vyāvartakam upalakṣaṇa viśeṣaṇam vā*[41] i.e neither *upalakṣaṇa* nor *viśeṣaṇa* is a distinguisher.

Naturally, by making such a statement he attracts all our attention towards him because it is apparently all contrary to what we have been discussing so far. But we are pacified by his next statement which is in reality the definitions of *viśeṣaṇa* and *upalakṣaṇa*. He says : *kāryāṅgam sat sambaddham viśeṣaṇam, kāryānaṅgam sat sambaddham ca upalakṣaṇam.*[42]

That is, that which is subsidiary to *kārya* and at the same time which is connected with the *viśeṣya* is called *viśeṣaṇa* and that which is not subsidiary and at the same time which is connected with *viśeṣya* is called *upalakṣaṇa*.

Naturally, it is evident from the definition that *vyāvartakatva* does not constitute the body of the definition. While explaining the reason for it, he points out that *vyavaccheda* or *vyāvṛtti* or differentiation is the purpose of both *viśeṣaṇa* and *upalakṣaṇa* and as such it need not enter into the text of the definition. Also because *vyāvṛtti* i.e. differentiation is common to both the concepts. Strictly speaking, in a definition, only *asādhāraṇadharma* i.e. unique property is to be stated as per the definition of definition.

Let us now see how the definition of *upalakṣaṇa* given by him applies to *prāśastya*. The sentence, *Vāyavyam śvetam ālabheta bhūtikāmaḥ* enjoins the *kāmya-paśuyāga*. And this sacrifice has been praised, through praising the deity by the *arthavāda* sentences, *'vāyur vai kṣepiṣṭhā devatā'* etc. Now, how to connect this praise with the *yāga* is a problem. That is solved by Murāri by saying that it is connected to *yāga* being an *upalakṣaṇa*. Let us see how it is connected to *yāga*.

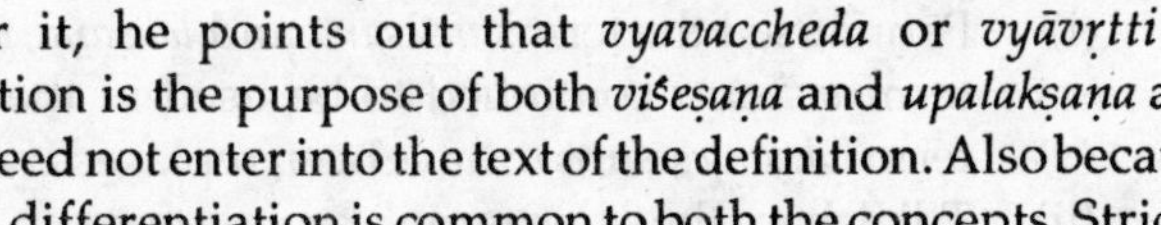

Devatā, which is praised, is directly connected with *yāga*, being the very form of *yāga*. But *prāśastya* being connected with the deity of that sacrifice directly, simply acts as a distinguisher of the *yāga* and is not connected with it directly. And thus becomes an indicator of *yāga*.

Thus, according to Murāri's concept, whether something is *upalakṣaṇa* or *viśeṣaṇa*, can be decided only in the context of an action. Say, for instance, in the expression, '*Kamaṇḍalunā chātram ānaya kamaṇḍalu* is *upalakṣaṇa* because it is not a subsidiary to the action of bringing, but it simply points to the student who is to be brought. If the speaker intends that the students should be brought along with the Kamaṇḍalu the normal expression would be '*Kamaṇḍalumantam chātram ānaya*' or '*Kamaṇḍalunā saha chātram ānaya*' and in that case the *Kamaṇḍalu* will be a *viśeṣaṇa*. But if it is simply, '*kamaṇḍalunā chātram ānaya*' then it is not necessary that the student should be brought along with the *Kamaṇḍalu* because that is not intended there.

(IV) Conclusion

(i) Pāṇni used the terms *viśeṣaṇa* and *lakṣaṇa, although* the term *viśeṣaṇa* continued to be used in that sense, the term *lakṣaṇa* seems to have been replaced by *upalakṣaṇa*.

(ii) Till Śabara the same term *lakṣaṇa* is used, in the sense of *cihna* i.e. a mark, but it is replaced by *upalakṣaṇa* from Kumārila onwards.

(iii) Prabhākara seems to be the first among the Mīmāṁsakas to attempt a definition of the term *upalakṣaṇa*.

(iv) Among the *Naiyāyikas*, it is Udayana who presented definitions for both *viśeṣaṇa* and *upalakṣaṇa*.

(v) Gaṅgeśa supplied a comprehensive definition of these concepts.

(vi) Murāri defined them with a different parameter, the hint of which he obtained from Prabhākra. To be precise, Murāri's concept of *Viśeṣaṇa* and *upalakṣaṇa* is different from that of the Bhāṭṭa school of *Mīmāṁsā* and the *Nyāya* school but it is closer to that of Prabhākara to the extent that both conceive these concepts in terms of action. Nevertheless, Murāri states them in clear terms with further specification by adding the qualification *sambaddha* to the respective definitions.

Note and References

1. e.g. the *Tattvacintamaṇi* of Gaṅgeśa, *Siddhānta muktāvali* of Viśvanātha etc.
2. This is an independent commentary on the *Jaimini Sūtras* (*JS*) 1.2.1; 1.2.31; 1.3.1; 1.3.24 and 1.4.1. The last two references were not mentioned in my book *Reconstruction of the Third School of Pūrvamīmāṁsā*, 'Satguru Publications, Sri Garib Dass Oriental Series no. 90, New Delhi, 1990, on pp. 11 and 96. In the light of this, the statement of M.M.G.N.Jha and Umesh Miśra stands correct (ibid, p. 11.).
3. *Na hi apratīte viśeṣaṇe viśiṣṭam kecana pratyetum arhanti*. *Śāharabhāṣya* on *JS*, 1.3.33. Edn., Anandasrama Sanskrit Granthavali, No. 97, pp. 247-48.
4. Vide *Śābarabhāṣya* on *JS* 1.3.33, ibid, p. 265.
5. Vide *Tantravārtika* on *Śābarabhāṣya* on *JS* 1.3.33, ibid, p. 265.
6. Ibid, p. 257.
7. Vide *Bṛhatī* of Prabhākara, edn, Madras University Sanskrit Series, No. 24, 1962, p. 165.
8. Ibid, p. 165.
9. Ibid, p.165.
10. Rjuvimaiā on *Bṛhatī*, ibid, p. 156.
11. *Bṛhatī* p. 166.
12. Ibid, p. 169.
13. Ibid, p. 164.
14. *Nāgṛhītaviśeṣaṇa viśiṣṭe buddhiḥ*, ibid, p. 173.
15. This work is referred to by Murāri very often.
16. Vide *Mīmāṁsānayaviveka*, edn. Rastriya Sanskrit Samsthanam, 1977, p. 156.
17. *Dharmāntareṇa vyāvṛttatayā dhīsthe dharmiṇi dharmāntaram Pratīyamanam upalakṣaṇam*, ibid, p. 156.
18. i.e. that of *dandī puruṣaḥ*, as explained above, ibid, p. 157.
19. Vide *Kraṇāvali*, edn. Gaekwad's Oriental Series, No. 154, p. 130.
20. The process is given as follows :
    apekṣābuddhi—dvittvotpatti—dvitvatva—dvitva-viṣayaka— nirvikalpaka—dvitvasavikalpaka—dvitva-Viśiṣṭa-dravya-savikalpaka.
    Vide *Vaiśeṣika-upaskāra*, edn., Haridas Sanskrit Granthamala, Vaisesika Vibhaga-3, No. 1, 1923, p. 176.
21. *viśeṣaṇam hi viśiṣṭa-jñāna-kāraṇam na tu viṣayaḥ*. Vide *kiraṇāvali*, p. 130.
22. *Tatha ca Viśiṣṭa-jñānotpattikale 'sato' pi pūrvabhāvinaḥ tattvamaviruddham*, ibid, p. 130.
23. Ibid, p. 130.
24. Ibid, p. 130.
25. Ibid, p. 130.
26. Vide *Saptapadārthī*, edn. Theosophical Publishing House, Adyar, Madras, 1932, pp. 149-150.
27. The influence of Grammar is quite apparent on this interpretation of Śivāditya Miśra.
28. Ibid, p. 149.
29. Ibid, p. 150.
30. These examples are offered by the commentator, ibid.
31. *Nāpi Viśeṣya-samāna-Vibhaktikatvam Viśeṣaṇatvam. Kākavat Devadattagṛhamityādau upalakṣaṇe' pi gatatvāt*. Vide *Tattvacintāmaṇi*, edn. Kendriya Sanskrit Vidyapith Granthamala, No. 20, 1973, p. 870.

32. *Ghaṭaḥ paṭaḥ ityabhidhānāt tayorapi anyonyaviśeṣaṇatāpāta ityapi bodhyam*, ibid, p. 870.
33. *Pṛtyāyya-vyāvṛtty adhikaraṇatā purusasya daṇḍena avacchidyate na puruṣatvena, ativyāpteḥ*, ibid, pp. 874-875.
34. *Upalakṣaṇe tu gṛhatāpasādiniṣṭha pratyāyya-vyāvṛtty adhikaraṇatā na kāka-jaṭādibhir-avacchidyate, tad-abhāvavaty-api vyāvṛtti-pratīteḥ*, ibid, p. 875.
35. *Evam ca pratyāyya-vyāvṛtty-dhikaraṇatā avacchedakatve sati vyāvartakam Viśeṣaṇam, tadanyavyāvartakam upalakṣaṇam*, ibid, p. 875.
36. Vide *Vyutpattivada*, edn. Chowkhamba Sanskrit Series Office, 1993. p. 233.
37. Viśeṣaṇasya saṁbandhaḥ matubādibhiḥ prattyāyyate, ibid, p. 234.
38. Ibid, p. 234.
39. Vide *Upaskāra*, p. 177.
40. Vide *Tripādīnītinayanam* of Murāri, Published in JORM, 1928.
41. Ibid.
42. Ibid.

6

Tātparya in Pūrvamimāṁsā

Kumārila Bhaṭṭa states in his *Tantravārtika* :

आकाङ्क्षा सन्निधानं च योग्यता चेति च त्रयम्।
सम्बन्धकारणत्वेन क्लृप्तं नानन्तरश्रुतिः ।।

Which means, expectancy, proximity and compatibility are the three causes of relationship (between word-meanings) and not merely the particular order of words (is the cause of sentence meaning.)

Mīmāṁsakas have formed various principles for the interpretation of Vedic sentences, the latter being their foremost task. As they have discussed the factors that decide the scope and nature of a sentence, they have also discussed the causal factors that are helpful in knowing the meaning of a sentence. In this context Kumārila has given three principles namely, *ākāṅkṣā, sannidhāna* and *yogyatā* to understand the relationship between two *padārthas* of word meanings which is nothing but sentence meaning. *Ākāṅkṣā* is expectancy. *Sannidhāna* is proximity (of time) and *yogyatā* is compatibility (of meanings). Let us see with the help of an example how these three work. Suppose, X utters one nominal form say राम : then it has an expectancy of some verbal form like *gacchati, paṭhati* or *pacati* to be with the tradition. Thus, one word namely *rāmaḥ* is not capable of expressing one complete meaning, and hence it expects another, i.e. some verbal form to express a complete sense. Similarly, if one word say, *rāmaḥ* is uttered now and another word say, *gacchati* after some lapse of time then also the two cannot make one sentence and cannot in turn produce an understanding of a complete meaning. These two are, thus, formal criteria which if not followed will not give rise to any single sentence and thereon to a complete meaning.

The third criterion namely *yogyatā* or compatibility is a semantic one and not formal one. To explain, if a traditional sentence, '*Vahninā siñcati* is uttered then even if the first two conditions are fulfilled, it will not generate any proper verbal understanding. Because the meaning of the word *vahni* cannot be connected with the meaning of the root *sic-siñc* as there is no compatibility between the two. So merely the formal criteria are not sufficient for the generation of verbal understanding. The semantic condition also has to be fulfilled. In its absence the result i.e. verbal cognition will not come into existence.

These are the three criteria given by the *Mīmāṁsakas* for the understanding of sentence meaning. They are later on accepted by other systems of Indian Philosophy also.

Naiyāyikas have added the fourth condition namely *tātparya* to the list of the three mentioned above. They have defined all these factors and their scope or role in producing verbal understanding. It seems that there is not so much of controversy so far as the roles of *ākāṅkṣā, sannidhāna* and *yogyatā* are concerned but *Mīmāṁsakas* do not see eye to eye with the *Naiyāyikas* so far as the role of tātparya is concerned.

Let us first survey the stand of the *Naiyāyikas* in brief so that the ground for objections and the point of view of the *Mīmāṁsakas* become more clear.

Naiyāyikas' Stand

Naiyāyikas have defined *tātparya* as *vakturicchā* which means literally, the desires of the speaker. We may translate it as the intention of the speaker as well, i.e. the desire of the speaker to convey certain meaning. To establish *tātparya* as a cause of verbal knowledge *Naiyāyikas* argue that if the intention of the speaker has no role to play in the generation of verbal cognition then it would have been difficult to understand either a horse or salt at different times from the same word '*saindhava*' in the sentence *saindhavaṁ ānaya*. Thus, according to them, when a speaker utters a sentence, '*saindhavam ānaya*' where one of the words carries two expressed meanings, the intention of the speaker helps the hearer get only one appropriate meaning. In other words, if the intention of the speaker is not known by the listener it is not possible for him to decide the meaning of the word because, in the absence of the knowledge of the intention of the speaker, both the meanings of the word will occur to his mind with same force and there will not be any criterion to select only one of them and behave consistently. Hence, conclude the *Naiyāyikas*, the role of *tātparya* is very significant in the process of verbal knowledge.

One may raise a question here : How about the Vedic sentences which do not have any speaker? In other words, how will he be able to know the purport of these sentences if he does not know the intention of the speaker who himself iṣ not known to him?

This has a very plain answer according to the *Naiyāyikas* : The Almighty God is the speaker so far as the sentences of the Vedas are concerned. In this case one cannot say that let the teacher of that particular Veda be considered as the speaker and thence let his intention be the cause of verbal understanding of the sentences of that particular Veda, because there was no teacher in the beginning of the creation. Whereas God is eternal—*anādi*—*ananta* who is the appropriate speaker of the all time valid Vedic sentence (vide *Śabdakhaṇḍa of Nyāyasiddhāntamuktāvali*).

It is obvious from this stand of the *Naiyāyikas* that the answer given by them to the question is very much in keeping with the framework of their system. We know that *Naiyāyikas* accept the creation and destruction of the universe for which they say there is Vedic support also. They have also accepted God as the creator of the Vedas along with the universe. Hence whatever they argue is befitting their logical and ontological frameworks.

There may arise a question about one more case of verbal behaviour and that is with parrot. How does a person understand a sentence uttered by a parrot? *Naiyāyikas* answer : only God's intention could be the cause of verbal knowledge from the sentence uttered by a parrot. If the sentences are not consistent, then? In other words, how does verbal understanding arise from the inconsistent sentences of the parrot? Because if God's intention is the cause accepted for verbal understanding from the parrot's sentences then they should never by insistent which is not a fact. In such cases, however, there is no other go than to accept that the intention of the teacher of the parrot is the cause there (ibid.).

This is, in brief, the stand of the Neologicians in general. But there is a section of the *Naiyāyikas* which believes that knowledge of the intention of the speaker does not play its role in each and every case of verbal understanding but it is necessary only when a sentence contains a polysemous word or words. This group of logicians believes that in case of the sentences of parrot verbal understanding arises without the knowledge of the intention of the speaker. And in case of Vedic sentences the rules of interpretation formed by the Mīmāṁsā system are the cause of the knowledge of them.

Mīmāṁsakas' Position

Mīmāṁsakas do not agree with the *Naiyāyikas* on this issue. It seems that the reason to this is mainly rooted in the basic differences between these two systems of Indian Philosophy.

Mīmāṁsakas have formed certain rules of interpretation for interpreting the Vedic sentences to which I have already referred before. One such principle is *prakaraṇa* which may generally be translated into Engligh as context. Basically this word *prakaraṇa* stands for 'topic' in the *Mīmāṁsā* system. 'Topic' means the main theme of a principal sentence. The *Mīmāṁsakas* explain : there is mutual expectancy between a *mukhyavidhi* and a *gauṇavidhi*. Because of this mutual expectancy these sentences i.e. the main injunction and the subordinate one form one single sentence i.e. *mahāvākya* as they refer to one single result. In other words their purpose being the same they are treated as a single sentence.

It is clear from this that here the word *prakaraṇa* means theme of the Vedic sentences. But if the meaning is extended a bit in the context of our verbal behaviour, it could mean the theme of our behaviour and then the context in which the verbal bahaviour takes place. Thus, *prakaraṇa* stands for the context or circumstances of a particular verbal behaviour. And hence the *Mīmāṁsakas* do not accept *tātparya* as an additional cause of verbal understanding. Whatever role *tātparya* plays in the process of verbal cognition according to the *Naiyāyikas* is taken care of by the principle of *prakaraṇa* according to the *Mīmāṁsakas*. The word *saindhava*, in the example of *saindhavam ānaya*, therefore, does convey the appropriate meaning to the listener, out of the two, on the basis of the circumstances in which the sentence is uttered. Suppose, it is uttered at the dining table none will get the meaning horse from the word and again, if it is uttered by a king who is all ready to leave on hunting or war the hearer will without fail understand horse from the same word *saindhava*. Here, according to the *Mīmāṁsakas*, context plays the significant role and therefore one is able to select the proper meaning of the word. Hence, *tātparya* as an additional cause for verbal understanding need not be accepted.

There is one more dimension to the problem for which *Mīmāṁsakas* are not prepared to accept the intention of the speaker as a producer of verbal knowledge and that is that they do not accept any speaker so far as the Vedic sentences are concerned. According to them, Vedas are *a-pauruṣeya*. There is no human association in their creation, and this is the reason why they are valid for ever.

If the concept of *tātparya* is accepted then how will verbal understanding arise from the Vedic sentences? To overcome this difficulty they have outright refuted the concept of *tātparya* which is so important for the *Naiyāyikas*. I have already stated before that these differences of opinion have their root in the basic tenets of both the systems.

Mīmāṁsakas have also used the word *tātparya* but not in the sense of the intention of the speaker. According to them, by implication, that which is the purport or purpose of the sentence is its *tātparya*. We may say, *yatparam vākyam tattasya tātparyam*. And this is treated as *prakaraṇa* or main so far as the sentence is concerned. Look at the verses of Śālikanātha :

भूयांसो यद्यपि स्वार्थाः पदानां ते पृथक् पृथक्।
प्रयोजनतया तु एकवाक्यार्थ सम्प्रचक्षते।।
तत्प्रतीत्येकाकार्यत्वाद् वाक्यमप्येकमुच्यते।
प्रतिपत्तिर्गुणानां हि प्रधानैकप्रयोजना।।

Here, the word *prayojana* stands for the purport of the sentence or that which is conveyed by the sentence as its content.

In this line, it is interesting to note how Murāri Miśra, the exponent of the third school of *Pūrvamīmāṁsā* (PM) feels about it. He in his *Arthavādādhikaraṇa* comments as follows : नैककप्रतीतिकारित्वमेकवाक्यतावधारणहेतुः किन्त्वेकार्थप्रतीतिपरत्वम्। तच्च प्रतीत्यजननेऽप्यस्ति। फलशून्यस्यापि तात्पर्यस्यानाप्तवाक्येष्विव सम्भवात्। (A Reconstruction of the Third School of PM by Ujjwala Panse, Garibdass Oriental Series No. 90, Sri Satguru Publications, New Delhi, 1990, p. 166).

Tr : The state of producing one understanding is not the ground for determining the sentence unity but it is the state of producing the understanding of one single object or purpose. And that (state of expressing knowledge of one object) is present even if there is no understanding just as it (the state of producing the understanding of one object) is found in the sentences of an unbelievable person where the result (i.e. successful activity) is not found. Thus, according to Murāri *tātparya* is *ekārthapratītiparatva* i.e. aiming at the knowledge of one purpose and he treats it as the cause of determining the sentence unity.

Observation

It becomes evident from whatever we have discussed so far that even if the *Naiyāyikas* accept *tātparya* as a necessary condition for the verbal understanding in case of all sentences, still when they come to an example they give it that of the sentence which contains a polysemous word. It seems from this that they are aware of the fact that actually it works effectively in such cases only.

From the stand of *Mīmāṁsakas* it is obvious why they are not prepared to accept *tātparya* to which I have already hinted. Nevertheless the later *Mīmāṁsakas* like Gāgābhaṭṭa have accepted almost everything proposed by the Naiyāyikas in this respect. *Bhāṭṭacintāmaṇi* observes, तात्पर्यं तु तत्प्रतीतीच्छया वक्त्रा अनुसंहितत्वम् । तत्र पदार्थतात्पर्यनिश्चयः संसर्गतात्पर्यनिश्चयश्च तादृशशाब्दबोधे हेतुः । .... शुकवाक्ये वेदवाक्ये चेश्वरतात्पर्यग्रहेण शाब्दबोधो अध्यापकतात्पर्येण वा । etc.

It is well known a fact that the later *Mīmāṁsakas* accepted God. It may be the reason why they accepted the view of the *Naiyāyikas* later. This is the reason why I say that the acceptance or non-acceptance of *tātparya* depends upon the acceptance or non-acceptance of God. Because verbal understanding arises both from the *laukika* and *vaidika* sentences alike. Hence the causes of both the effects should be of a similar type. If in the case of *laukika* sentences the speaker's i.e. some human being's desire is to be accepted as a cause then there should also be someone, be it the God, in case of Vedic sentences whose desire acts as the cause of verbal understanding there.

We have also seen how *Mīmāṁsakas* have used the word *tātparya* in a different sense than in which it is used by the

Naiyāyikas. While *Prābhākaras* have used it in the sense of main theme of the sentence, Murāri has treated it as the cause of determining sentence unity.

References

1. *Tantravārtika* of Kumārila Bhaṭṭa, Anandashram Sanskrit Series No. 97, Anandashram, Pune.
2. *Nyāya-Siddhāntamuktāvali* of Viśvanātha Nyāyapañcānana, The Kashi Sanskri Series No. 6, Chowkhamba Sanskrit Series Office, Varanasi, 1972.
3. *Prakaraṇapañcācikā* of Śālikanātha Miśra, Benares Hindu University Darśana Series, No. 4, Banares Hindu University Varanasi, 1961.
4. *Arthavādādhikaraṇa* of Murāri Miśra vide *A Reconstruction of the Third School of Pūrvamimāṁsā*, by Ujjwala Panse, Sri Garibdass Oriental Series, No. 90, Sri Satguru Publications, New Delhi, 1990.
5. *Bhāṭṭacintāmaṇi* of Gāngābhaṭṭa, with the Comm. *Mayūkka*; Ed. by S.N. Shukla, (Part I and II), 1933 and 1938.

7

Prābhākaras' Concept of Kārya

Prābhākara concept of Kārya is much discussed a concept in the system of *Pūrvamīmāṁsā* (*PM*) because it is an important postulation of an intermediate causal link (*apūrva*) between the performance of *yāga* (sacrifice) and its result (*i.e.* heaven etc.). The primary meaning of the word which is common to the classical Sanskrit language is, 'something to be done or something to be established by an action'. This meaning is extended by particularly the Prābhākara *Mīmāṁsakas* to the meaning of the causal link between a sacrifice and its result as mentioned above.

In this paper, an attempt is made to survey the arguments of the *Prābhākaras* in defence of their concept of *kārya*, and to draw a picture of the same as clear as possible.

Kārya is a very important concept for the *Prābhākaras* as it is the main incentive for a person on the knowledge of which he is prompted to take up an action. *Prābhākaras* (*Prā*) argue that it is not sufficient to know the action or the result or merely the relation between the two. Because even if the relation between the action and the result namely, *sādhana-sādhyabhāva* is known one is not prompted to take up that particular action. As is seen in case of taking food and satisfaction which took place in the past etc. But when one knows the *kāryatā* one is prompted towards taking up that activity. In other words, when one knows 'this is my *kārya*' *i.e.* I have to do this—one is prompted.

This *kārya* is expressed by the suffix *liṅ* with the expression of *kṛti;* i.e. *liṅ* expresses *kṛti* as well as *kārya*. Because, Śālikanātha clarifies, *kārya* is very much connected with *kṛti* and hence it is not possible that *kṛti* is not expressed (by a particular word) but *kārya* is expressed. In other words, if *kṛti* is not expressed, *kārya* will not be expressed (vide *prakaraṇa Pañcikā* (*PP*), p. 426.

After explaining the stand of Prā. in this way, Śālikanātha comes to the doubt raised by the Bhāṭṭas (*Bhā.*) i.e. particularly by

Maṇḍana Miśra. the question is this : It is accepted that the knowledge of *kāryatā* alone prompts a person (into an action) but what exactly is this *kāryatā*? It seems that this *kāryatā* is nothing but *iṣṭasādhanatā*. *Iṣṭasādhanatā* is expressed by the *vidhiliṅ* and the same is the cause of inducement. Śālikanātha has quoted the view of Maṇḍana Miśra in the following :

अपेक्षितोपायेनैव विधिरिष्टो मनीषिभिः ।
अतो हयध्यवसायादिर्नाऽकस्मान्नाऽभिधानतः ।।

and also in the following :

पुंसो नेष्टाभ्युपायत्वात् क्रियास्वन्यः प्रवर्तकः ।
प्रवृत्तिहेतुं धर्मञ्च प्रवदन्ति प्रवर्तनाम् ।। विधिविवेक 29
कर्तुरिष्टाभ्युपाये हि कर्तव्यमिति लोकधीः ।
विपरीते त्वकर्तव्यामिति तद्विषये ततः ।। -विधिकविवेक 30

Thus, Maṇḍana Miśra's intention is very clear—he says when a person knows that such and such an instrument will lead to the result desired by him he thinks that he should go for that instrument and vice-versa. Hence *iṣṭasādhanatā* is the meaning of the *liṅ* suffix and that itself is the cause of the inducement. Thus, he wants to suggest that what the *Prā*. are calling *kāryatā* the same is named by the *Bhā*. as *iṣṭasādhanatā* and hence there is no difference between the two. The difference is only in names.

The doubt of the *Bhā*. is thoroughly answered by Śālikanātha. He directly denies the identity between *kāryatā* and *phalasādhanatā* suggested by Maṇḍana Miśra. He argues, the two are different because in past things there exists *iṣṭasādhanatā* but that cannot be treated as *kāryatā*. Inducement also is not possible only on the basis of the *iṣṭasādhanatā*. He observes :

फलसाधनता नाम या सा नैव च कार्यता।
कार्यता कृतिसाध्यत्वं फलसाधनता पुनः ।। 7 ।।
करणत्वं फलोत्पादे भिद्येते ते परस्परम् ।। (PP. p.428)

and further adds :

यद्यप्येकवस्तुनिवेशिता द्वयोः तथापि स्वरूपभेदोऽस्त्येव । तदेव हि वस्तु फलं प्रत्युपायभावात् फलसाधनमित्युच्यते, कृत्यधीनात्मलाभतया च कार्यमिति । (ibid, p. 428)

Thus, according to Śālikanātha *kāryatā* is none other than *kṛtisādhyatā* and *iṣṭasādhanatā* is an instrumentality towards the production of the effect (which is desired). What he says is the same thing can become *phalasādhana* when it is instrumental in bringing about the result and when it attains itself through *kṛti* it is called *kārya*. Thus, even if there is a possibility of these two properties namely *kāryatā* and *iṣṭasādhanatā* existing in one and the same thing, still, they differ in their nature i.e. they are not identical with each other as proposed by the *Bhā*.

The doubt here is three-fold as we can see from the above description : (1) Whether the knowledge of *iṣṭasādhanatā* acts as the cause of inducement (*pravṛtti*) or (2) it is the knowledge of *kāryatā* which plays this role or (3) The two (i.e. *iṣṭasādhanatā* and *kāryatā*) are not at all different?

Śālikanātha has clarified his intention quite elaborately. The first alternative is not acceptable because *iṣṭasādhanatā* is present in the things which have already occurred or which are yet to occur i.e. the things of past and future but there no *pravṛtti* is seen and so it is not only the knowledge of *iṣṭasādhanatā* that induces a person into an action but he needs to know that something is *kṛtisādhya i.e.* achievable by his efforts over and above his knowledge that something will lead to the result desired by him. Śālikanātha declares that this *kṛtisādhyatā* is *kāryatā*. So it is the second alternative that is acceptable to *Prā*. It also rules out the possibility of the third one. (comm. on *PP*., p. 428-9)

Another question that arises here is : Whether this *kāryatā* or *kartavyatā* is known only in case of the means of a desired object (*iṣṭasādhanatā*) or it is known with reference to (any) other activities also. Śālikanātha replies : a particular activity achieves the status of *kārya* only when *phalasādhanatā* in that particular thing is known. In other words *phalasādhanatā* always precedes *kāryatā* i.e. the knowledge of the *phalasādhanatā* is the cause of the knowledge of *kāryatā*. To explain, as a general rule the activities of man lead him to unhappiness. Therefore, when a person knows that something is going to lead him to happiness, say, in the form of heaven—he comes to know the *kāryatā* residing in that something.

To quote *PP* :

किन्तु स्वयं क्लेशरूपं कर्म यत्कार्यतां व्रजेत् ।
फलसाधनता तत्र कारणं तेन कार्यता ।।

तद्भावभाविनी नित्यं तदा सैव प्रकाशते।
स्वभावेन हि कर्माणि दुःखोत्पादहेतुभूतानि।
तेषु कार्यत्वावगमः फलसाधनतावगमनिबन्धनः। (ibid, p.429)

To describe the nature of *kāryatā* Śālikanātha states : *kāryatā* is not only the achievement (of the *iṣṭa*) through *kṛti* but is something main or principle to the *kṛti* which is its subsidiary. And this alone is the cause of inducement.

कार्यमेव हि सर्वत्र प्रवृत्तावेककारणम्।
कृतिसाध्यं प्रधानं यत् तत्कार्यमभिधीयते। (ibid, p. 429)

After describing the nature of *kārya* as exactly as possible, next important issue is how this *kāryatā* is known? What are the means to know the *kāryatā* residing in a particular *iṣṭasādhanatā*? The answer is, by perception and inference. Śālikanātha explains, *kārya* is nothing but the aim or object of *kṛti* and it is *pradhāna* or principal to the *kṛti* is nothing but *prayatna* or effort of a person. Thus, *prayatna* is known by mental perception, and *prayatnasādhyatā* i.e. *kṛtisādhyatā* i.e. *kāryatā* is known by an inference. Because there is invariable concomitance between *kṛti* and *kāryatā*. *Kāryatā* can be there only when *kṛti* is there and vice-versa. Śālikanātha says :

कृतौ सत्यां भावात्, असत्यान्चाभावदनुमानतः कृतिसाध्यता तावदवगम्यते। यदधिकृत्य कृतिः प्रवर्तते तत्कृतेः प्रधानम्। प्रयत्नश्च कृतिः। स च मानसप्रत्यक्षवेद्य इति.... तेन प्रत्यक्षानुमानाभ्यां कार्यम् अवगम्यते। (ibid, pp. 431-32)

To establish his stand that *kārya* is expressed by the suffix *liṅ* Śālikanātha argues : as one comes to know an expressed meaning of a word on the basis of *āvāpa-udvāpa* so also it can be understood that *kārya* is the expressed meaning of a *liṅ* suffix on the basis of *āvāpa* and *udvāpa*.

शब्दान्तराणि स्वार्थेषु व्युत्पद्यन्ते यथैव हि।
आवापोद्वापभेदेन तथा कार्ये लिङादयः।। (ibid, p.430)

and also :

.....। तत्रापि कोऽर्थः केन शब्देनाभिहित इति विवेचने लिङाद्यावापे कार्यावगतिदर्शनात् तदुद्धारे चादर्शनात् त एव कार्यावगतिं कुर्वन्तीति शब्दान्तरवल्लिङादीनां कार्यवाचकत्वव्युत्पत्तिसिद्धिः। (ibid, p.430)

Here, if it is the case that *liṅ* expresses *kārya* then a question is raised by some that when a sentence containing a *liṅ* suffix is heard, it is observed by the people in our day-to-day behaviour that some (performance of an) action takes place and hence it is proper to say that *kārya* (expressed by *liṅ*) is nothing but some action (*kārya*) because *avagati* and *pravṛtti i.e.* knowledge and inclination should refer to one and the same object as a person does not go to take up some other action when he understands *kāryatā* in something else.

Prābhākaras accept this suggestion and argue that so far as everyday activities are concerned *kārya* is nothing but an action but in case of Vedic sentences it cannot be so. Because an action is transient thing and thence it is not possible on its part to remain present at the time when the effect comes into existence. Because in many cases the time when an effect of a sacrificial performance takes place is very distant future from the time of the actual performance. Neither can it be connected with the *niyojya* for the same reason. Hence, in case of the Vedic sentences it is *kārya* only which is expressed by the suffix *liṅ*. The nature of this *kārya* is already stated by Śālikanātha that it is achieved through *kṛti* and it is the means of the desired result namely heaven etc. To sum up, though in case of *laukika vyavahāra* it is possible to identify an action with *kārya*—as the *laukika* action yields the result instantly, say, for example an action of kindling a lamp immediately brings about the effect expected from it namely getting light. In case of Vedic sentences however *kārya* is never identical with the transient action. It is very much different from it, being more durable than the same and being fit to be related with the *Niyojya*.

तस्मान्नियोज्यसम्बन्धसमर्थं विधिवाचिभिः।
कार्यं कालान्तरस्थायि क्रियातो भिन्नमुच्यते।। (ibid, p.436)

The same *kārya* is sometimes called by the name *apūrva* or *niyoga*. It is called *apūrva* because it is not known by any other means of knowing before (the Vedic injunction is heard). And the same is sometimes called *niyoga* because it prompts the *niyojya* towards itself in the form of *kārya*.

क्रियादिभिन्नं यत्कार्यं वेद्यं मानान्तरैर्न तत्।
अतो मानान्तरापूर्वमिति गीयते।। (ibid, p.441)

and also,

कार्यत्वेन नियोज्यञ्च स्वात्मनि प्रेरयन्नसौ।
नियोग इति मीमांसानिष्णातैरभिधीयते।। (ibid, p. 441)

Observations

From whatever we have discussed so far the picture of *kārya* according to *Prābhākaras* that we can draw is, in short, as follows :

(1) *Kārya* is not *yāga* (sacrifice) or any performance but it is something to be achieved by performing that particular action which ultimately leads to the desired result. Thus, it is produced by a performance of *yāga* and in turn produces the desired result i.e. heaven etc. at a proper time. In other words, it is *kṛtisādhya* and *kāmyasādhaṇa* (*PP.*, p. 431 and 433).

(2) The means to know *kārya* is either *pratyakṣa* or *anumāna*.

(3) The word that expresses *kārya* is the suffix *liṅ* i.e. an optative suffix. This can be known through *āvāpa* and *udvāpa* of the suffix *liṅ*.

(4) The meaning of *liṅ* is known as *praiṣa* in case of the common parlance. To explain, when a senior person uses an optative suffix in a sentence addressed to a junior one that suffix *liṅ* generally expressed a *praiṣa* i.e. an order or a command. *Prakaraṇapañcikā* clarifies that this *praiṣa* (or *āmantraṇa* or *adhyeṣaṇā* in the context of *sama*—similar or *kanīyasa i.e.* junior persons) is nothing but a different name for the same *kārya*. In other words, the *kārya* is varily called by the name of *praiṣa* etc. in different contexts.

(5) So far as our day-to-day behaviour is concerned, *Prābhākaras* have accepted that *liṅ* expresses some action or *kārya* only. In other words, in our common parlance *kārya* stands for an action.

(6) In Vedic context, however, *kārya* cannot mean merely an action. It is very much different from the transient action as it is more durable than it and ultimately produces the final result. Thus, it behaves like an intermediate *vyāpāra* which is produced by the sacrifice and which in turn produces the final result of sacrifice at a proper time.

8

A Note on Prābhākara Theory of Śābdabodha

We express our experience through the medium of language. Language is a collection of sentences and sentences are collections of words. When a sentence is uttered by a speaker, it causes an understanding in the hearer. This understanding in the hearer is called verbal understanding.

Two questions may arise here :

(1) What actually is verbal understanding and (2) How does it take place. Answer to the former is simpler and not controversial. Verbal understanding is knowledge of the meaning of a sentence and the knowledge of sentence-meaning is not merely knowledge of word-meaning. This knowledge has an object in the form of the relations between word-meanings.

However, the latter being controversial is discussed by the Indian philosophers in details.

The process of verbal understanding can be generally described in the following way :

(i) *Padajñāna*—First one acquires the knowledge of words (by reading or hearing a sentence).
(ii) *Padārthasmaraṇa*—Then remembers the meaning of the words (for this step that the hearer knows the language in which the sentence is uttered is taken for granted).
(ii) *Tātparyajñāna*—Then the intention of the speaker is known.
(iii) *Śādabodha*—Then the verbal understanding takes place.

The phenomenon that the 'very fact' is understood by the hearer as it was expressed by the speaker can be explained as the words are expressive of definite meanings to a certain extent. In other words, this phenomenon presupposes a fixed or regular type of relation between a word and its meaning generally. *Naiyāyikas* call this relation by the name *vṛtti* i.e. *śakti* and *lakṣaṇā* whereas the *Mīmāṁsakas* hold that the words have *śakti* i.e. capacity to denote certain meanings, as according to them each and everything in this universe possesses a capacity to perform some function or the other.

To come to our point, when a sentence is heard, the hearer understands the meanings of all the constituent words of the sentence. But this knowledge of the meanings of all the constituent words of the sentence cannot be called an understanding of sentence-meaning because this knowledge is nothing more than the knowledge of word-meanings. Then what is the understanding of sentence-meaning? The connection among the meanings expressed by the words of the sentence is called sentence meaning and understanding of this sentence-meaning is called verbal understanding.

Here, a question arises : How these relations among word meanings are known? i.e. wherefrom do we obtain these relations? Answers to this question vary and stand for various independent theories of verbal understanding, in Indian philosophy. Among these theories the *saṁsargamaryādāvāda* of the Naiyāyikas, *Abhihitānvayavāda* of the Bhāṭṭa Mīmāṁsakas and *anvitābhidhānavāda* of the Prābhākara Mīmāṁsakas are well-known.

This paper intends to examine the stand of *Prābhākaras* by taking into account the objections of the *Naiyāyikas* against it with special reference to *Śaśadhara*—the author of *Nyāyasiddhāntadīpa*. I have also tried to point out the extent of the area of application of the Prābhākaras stand.

Let us first see in brief what exactly the *Anvitābhidhānavāda* is. *Anvitābhidhāna* literally means expression of connected or related (*anvitasya abhidhānam*). According to *Prābhākaras*, a word does not denote any meaning in isolation but it denotes its meaning as connected with the other meaning i.e. an action. In other words, *Prābhākaras'* intention is that words express the meaning of a sentence and it is not the case that either a sentence or the word-meanings convey it.

To make it clear, when a sentence is heard, knowledge of the relations among the meanings of the constituents of that particular sentence is generated in the hearer. There is no difference of opinion over this. But the question is, what is the linguistic element in the sentence from which this knowledge of the relations is derived? In other words, there has to be some controlling factor in the absence of which one cannot explain the fact that a particular sentence produces a particular verbal understanding. What is that controlling factor? It could either be the *padaśakti* i.e. the capacity of words or *arthaśakti* i.e. the capacity of the meanings expressed by them. *Prābhākaras* argue that since there is logical simplicity in accepting that the words have this capacity, it is proper to hold that words express sentence-meaning.

Another reason to hold such a view is that unless we accept that the relation is also expressed by a word, the *ākāṅkṣā* or expectancy to know the other part of the sentence cannot be explained. Because if the general relation is not known, there is no possibility of the desire to know the specific relation. To explain, if we divide a sentence into two parts namely, *kāraka* word and a *kriyā* word then if the *kāraka* word is known there should not be any expectancy to know the *kriyā* unless the relation also is known from the *kāraka* word and vice versa.

A doubt may be raised here that if the word expresses its meaning and relation also then the other word in the sentence will become redundant. But this contingency has no scope because, the other word is as much necessary as it will make one know the counter relatum (*pratiyogin*) of that relation.

Naiyāyikas' Stand and Objections Against the Prābhākaras

Before we go to the objections of the *Naiyāyikas* against the *Prābhākaras* let us see in brief what is their theory of *śābdabodha*. Their theory is known by the name *saṁsargamaryādāvada*. According to this theory, when a sentence is heard, the word-meanings are understood from the constituent words and the relations among the word-meaning are obtained only from the juxtaposition of those particular words. In other words, the particular order in which the words are presented in the sentence gives rise to the knowledge of the relations among the word-meanings. Thus, according to them, neither the words nor the word-meanings give rise to the understanding of the sentence-meaning but this function is performed by the juxtaposition of particular words.

Objections Against the Prābhākaras

The main question of the *Naiyāyikas* on this is whether the relation in general is expressed by the word or the specific relation is expressed. If the former alternative is correct then the fault of sentence-split will be unavoidable because in that case we will have two different verbal understandings arising from the same sentence namely (i) the *kāraka* is related with an action and (ii) the action is related with the *kāraka*. It is well known that the fault of sentence-split (*vākyabheda*) is a serious one and has to be avoided so far as possible according to the *Mīmāṁsakas*.

Not only this but the specific action or the specific *kāraka* will also remain unknown and hence the specific meaning of the sentence also will not be understood.

If juxtaposition of the words along with the expectancy is the solution to the problem i.e. the means to know the specific sentence-meaning then the *Naiyāyikas* argue that when it is possible to explain the knowledge of relation from the juxtaposition of the words, it is not proper to say that the word expresses it.

If the latter alternative is acceptable to *Prābhākaras* namely a word expresses specific relation then the sentence-meaning is known from a word itself and hence the other words in the sentence become redundant.

The argument that unless we accept that the relation in general is expressed by the word, the desire to know the specific relation cannot be explained, is also not tenable according to the Naiyāyikas. They say that the invariable relation between a *kāraka* and *kriyā* is sufficient to know the relation in general and that explains the desire to know the specific relatum.

Śaśadhara in his famous work *Nyāyasiddhāntadīpa* has further given an interesting example to refute the above-said theory. He says if on seeing a *jambīra* fruit (citron) one has a desire to know the particular taste of that *jambīra*, on the basis of this desire we will have to accept that the taste of *jambīra* in general is also known by the eyes. Because as per the theory, unless general taste is known desire to know the particular taste cannot be claimed to have any scope.

In short *naiyāyikas'* stand could be stated like this : since the verbal understanding cannot take place unless there is relation between two word-meanings and since this relation can be known by other means, the words express only that meaning which cannot be known by any other means. Śaśadhara has recorded the following verse in this connection :

अन्वयस्यान्यतः प्राप्तेरन्यथाऽनुपपत्तितः ।
अनन्यलभ्यमात्रार्थशक्तान्येव पदानि नः ।।

Moreover, if it is accepted that the words express the relation then the relation between the word-meanings will become prominent and the counter-relatum will be subordinate to it which is not a fact. On the contrary we understand the counter-relatum as prominent one and the relation as subordinate to it.

It is well known that *Vṛddhavyavahāra* is acceptable also to the *Naiyāyikas*. They accept it as one of the means for knowing the relation between a word and its meaning (vide *Śabdakhaṇḍa* of *Siddhāntamuktāvali*).

Observations

From all that we have discussed so far it is evident that the *Prābhākaras* and the *Naiyāyikas* are interpreting the general rule "*ananyalabhyaḥ śabdārthaḥ*" in two different ways. While the *Prābhākaras* are thinking that each and every element in the *śābdabodha* must be had from some linguistic element in the sentence from which the *śābdabodha* has arisen, the *Naiyāyikas* do not agree with them. They argue that meaning in the *śābdabodha* which can be had by any other means should not be the meaning of a word i.e. a word should express that meaning which cannot be obtained from any other source. In other words, Prābhākaras have treated the word `*śabda*' in the rule `*ananyalabhyaḥ śabdārthaḥ*' to be *śabdapramāṇa*, the means of valid knowledge whereas *Naiyāyikas* have taken it to mean simply a word.

It can be further observed that the theory of *Prābhākaras* is well acceptable at the stage of first language learning where a child learns a language by observing the *vṛddhavyavahāra* i.e. the behaviour of the elder persons where each and every word is understood invariably in connection with some action or the other, hence activity or action plays a very important role at this stage. But at the stage of second language learning one cannot argue on the side of the *Prābhākaras* since one has to know the parts of speech distinctly at this state.

The theory of *anvitābhidhāna* is also applicable while acquiring the knowledge of the relation between a word and its meaning initially. We know that this fact is accepted by the *Naiyāyikas* also. Thus, we may conclude that the theory is applicable in the above-said cases but not in case of the verbal understanding in general.

---

* This chapter is mainly based on the *anvayaśaktinirāsavāda* of Śaśdhara in the *Nyāyasiddhāntadīpa* (Ed. B.K. Matilal, L.D. series 56, L.D. Institute of Indology, Ahmedabad-9).

9

Prābhākaras on Negation

'Negation' is one of the most controversial topics in Indian philosophy. There are almost as many views on this topic as many philosophers. The Naiyāyikas treat it as an object of true cognition i.e. *prameya*. They accept that it is perceived through sense-organs and we all know that later the Naiyāyikas have accepted it as an independent entity. Bhāṭṭa Mīmāṁsakas not only accept it as *prameya* but according to them since it is a different kind of *prameya* it requires different type of *pramāṇa* to cognise it, and hence they accept *abhāva* or absence as an object of true cognition and also accept *anupalabdhi* as *pramāṇa* or means to cognise this special kind of object.

Prābhākara Mīmāṁsakas on the other hand reject the possibility of accepting *abhāva* as a separate category of entity. They say, for explaining the behaviour of or with absence one need not accept it as an independent entity-hence accepting the *anupalabdhi-pramāṇa* is out of question-since there is no object to cognise through it.

Naiyāyikas have raised several questions and objections regarding this stand of Prābhākaras. In this paper, I propose to discuss the possible answers of the Prābhākaras to certain questions of the Naiyāyikas and try to evaluate them.

It will be helpful to understand the problem if we look into the basic stands of these two systems of Indian Philosophy namely, Nyāya system of Indian Philosophy and Prābhākara school of *Pūrvamīmāṁsā* regarding Negation. Accordingly, the paper is divided into four parts : (1) Prābhākaras' position, (2) Naiyāyikas' stand and Objections against Prābhākaras (3) Answer of the Prābhākaras, and (4) Conclusion.

(1) Prābhākaras' position

We have seen that Prābhākaras do not accept *abhāva*. In other words, there is nothing called negative entity but what is called so by other system is merely a positive entity for the Prābhākaras. According to them knowledge of positive entities is of two types : (1) Knowledge having an object in the form of positive entity connected with some other entity and (2) Knowledge having an object in the form of one single positive entity. The second case is the case of *abhāva. Śalikanātha* explains : There are two types of counterpositives (*Pratiyogins*) : visible and invisible. When a counterpositive is visible and there arises knowledge of second type i.e. that of one single positive entity-that is to be treated as *abhāva* of that counterpositive e.g. pot (*ghaṭa*) is a visible counterpositive and if one has knowledge only of a piece of ground (*bhūtala*) then that is to be treated as *abhāva* of *ghaṭa*. Hence the verbal understanding arising from the sentence *'bhūtale ghaṭaḥ nāsti'* is *'ghaṭe dṛśye bhūtalamātrasya bodhaḥ'* which means: when the pot is visible i.e. the counterpositive is a visible object, only the piece of ground is cognised.

Thus, when a counterpositive, say *ghaṭa*, is visible, and one has knowledge of one single object, say *bhūtala*, then that knowledge is specially expressed in the sentence, *'bhūtale ghaṭābhāvaḥ'*.

Śālikanātha further adds that even those who accept *abhāva* as an object of true cognition (*prameya*) also have to accept this 'knowledge having one single positive entity as its object' because they also have to accept *dṛśyādarśana* i.e. not visualising something which is visible-(we know that Naiyāyikas call it *'yogyānupalabdhi'*) as the means to know *abhāva* because without a means knowledge will not come into existence. Hence where the Naiyāyikas accept *abhāva* in that locus they also have to accept *dṛśyādarśana* and this *dṛśyādarśana* is fixed by perceiving one single object out of the two equally visible objects. Therefore, it is adequate to accept, *'dṛśye pratiyogini tadekaviṣayā upalabdhi'* as *abhāva*.

A question may be raised here that if *abhāva* is not accepted then how the knowledge of one single entity arises where previously knowledge of connected entities was there? If *pradhvamsābhāva* is accepted then it is possible to explain such knowledge.

Prābhākara's reply is : the same question could be put to them who accept *pradhvaṁsa*, that where there was presence of something say *ghaṭa* how does in the same place absence of the same thing occur? If the answer is, by some cause like *mudgarapāta* i.e. hammering it, then what on the earth can prevent one to have the knowledge of single entity by the same cause? However, one should remember in this case that *vināśa* or destruction is not the cause accepted by the Prābhākaras but they call it *bhāvāntarodaya* i.e. arising of a different positive entity. This *bhāvāntarodaya* also should be understood in the sense of *'dharmiṇahsvarūpamātreṇāvasthānam'* i.e. existence of a substratum in itself and if you ask what this *svarūpa* is, the answer is *ekākī bhāvaḥ* i.e. one single positive entity. Knowledge of this *ekaki bhāva* is the cause of the knowledge of *abhāva* and even without the knowledge of *abhāva* the *svarūpamātra* of the thing is cognised and hence *itaretarābhāva* is expressed by the word *mātra*.

Finally, mere knowledge of one single entity is not treated as *abhāva* but 'dṛśye *pratiyogini yā tadekaviṣayā buddhiḥ sā tadabhāvaḥ*'- which we have already discussed. Hence, the sentence *bhūtale ghaṭo nāsti* gives arise to an understanding *dṛśye' pi ghaṭe bhūtalamātram upalabhyate* and this knowledge is self-illuminating and does not require any other *pramāṇa* to know it.

(2) Naiyāyikas' Stand and the Objections against Prābhākaras

Let us now turn to the Naiyāyikas. Naiyāyikas have accepted absence as a *prameya*-object of true knowledge. It has to be accepted because we have true knowledge of it and that the knowledge is true can be decided by the facts that (1) it is not contradicted by any other knowledge and (2) it generates fruitful behaviour. Naiyāyikas do not need *anupalabdhi pramāṇa* to cognise *abhāva* but according to them it is perceived where *Yogyānupalabdhi* is a helping factor and their general rule says : *yena indriyeṇa yad gṛhyate tadgatā jātiḥ tad abhāvas' cāpi tenaiva indriyeṇa gṛhyete'* which means : whatever is perceived by a sense organ, its universal as well as it absence is also perceived by the same sense organ.

Main arguments of them regarding the necessity of accepting *abhāva* as an independent entity are as follows : as the sentence *bhūtale ghaṭaḥ* 'there is a pot on the ground' expresses some positive meaning i.e. 'the pot possess the superstratumness described by the substratumness existing in that particular piece of ground', similarly, the sentence *bhūtale ghaṭaḥ nāsti* conveys exactly opposite of it i.e. the negative fact namely, absence of pot possesses the superstratumness described by the substratumness existing in the ground etc. As each of the constituents of the first sentence refers to some particular referent, each and every constituent of the second sentence also should refer to some referent existing in the external world which is real. Why? Because the definition of word offered by the Naiyāyikas is *śaktam padam* which means *Śaktiviśiṣṭam padam*. *Śakti* is a relation between a word and its meaning. That which possesses the *śakti* i.e. the relation with meaning is called word or *pada*. If *'na'* is a word, it has to refer to some referent which exists externally in this world-and that referent is *abhāva* according to them, hence the sentence *bhūtale ghaṭaḥ na* conveys the absence of pot on a particular piece of ground. this also explains the *ādhārādheyabhāva* between the referent of the word *'bhūtala* and the referent of the word *'na'*.

Objections Against the Prābhākaras

Now let us proceed to the main objections raised by the Naiyāyikas against the Prābhākaras.

If *abhāva* is not accepted as an independent entity and as the referent of *nañ* then : (1) the first thing you are denying is the experience of the common man who behaves with absence without getting betrayed by his knowledge of it. In other words the consistent behaviour with *abhāva* remains unexplained. (2) The *ādhārādheyabhāva* remains unexplained (3) If *abhāva* isnot accepted, one can infer two horns on the head of a hare or the bristle on the skin of the tortoise. and (4) The main question goes unanswered : what is the referent to which *nañ* refers?

(3) Answer of the Prābhākaras

Of all the these objections the last one is most pertinent here but before we come to it we shall see in brief the answers to the other questions.

The first question is about the consistent behaviour of a common man with *abhāva*.

Prābhākaras say that there is no difficulty in explaining the behaviour of *abhāva* because we also accept *abhāva-vyavahāra*. Because even if *abhāva* is not accepted, the consistent behaviour can be easily explained. We do accept *vyavahāra* of *abhāva* or *vināśa* but the nature of *abhāva* and the nature of *vināśa* are different for us. According to our view *abhāva* is of the nature of *tadekaviṣayā buddhiḥ* i.e. knowledge of the single positive entity-and *vināśa* is of the nature of *bhāvāntarodaya*. This explains the consistent behaviour all the same. One should remember here that the controversy is not regarding the terms, namely न अ— -etc. but it is regarding the referent of these terms. (2) Second question was about the *ādhārādheyabhāva* between the referent of the word *bhūtala* and that of '*na*'.

Even if we do not accept *abhāva* as a *prameya*, the knowledge of *ādhārādheyabhāva* is not hampered. It will be explicit when we come to discuss the last question. (3) Third question was about inferring the horns of the hare and bristle on the skin of tortus.

This is ridiculous in as much as, inference cannot operate unless all factors for its operation are present. Moreover, it is not possible to infer anything anywhere, because the nature of *abhāva* is that of single positive entity-when a *pratiyogin* is visible.

(4) Let us now turn to the last question i.e. what is the referent of nañ? In other words, what will be the verbal understanding arising from the sentence *bhūlate ghaṭaḥ nāsti* or *bhūtalam ghaṭaḥ na* according to Prābhākaras?

The answer of the Prābhākaras is : the word *nāsti*' refers to *adhikaraṇamātra. Hence the understanding arising from the sentence 'bhūlate ghaṭaḥ nāsti'* will be *'bhūtale ghaṭādhikaraṇatva*-mātram. If we analyse it further, it will come to something like this :

भूतलनिष्ठ–आधारतानिरुपित–आधेयतावत् घटाधिकरणत्वमात्रम्

Which means : the superstratumness in mere State of being the locus of pot is described by the substratumness existing in the ground.

It is evident from this that the above-discussed *ādhārādheyabhāva* is not hampered at all.

In case of अन्योन्याभाव when the sentence is भूतलं घटः न the sentence-meaning will be भूतलघटस्वरुपमात्रम् because here 'न' stands for स्वरुपमात्रम्. It can further be paraphrased as भूतलस्वरुपमात्रम्–घटस्वरुपमात्रम्

(4) Conclusion

It is felt that the answer of the Prābhākaras are to a great extent satisfactory. But it always has happened that Naiyāyikas explain any behaviour by taking into account the common man's language and hence their theory seems to be more acceptable. Here also they argue that the word 'न' must stand for negative entity since the common man's behaviour reckons to it. Of course, they have justified their stand logically.

Further, what is achieved by the Prābhākaras by not accepting *abhāva* is very clear : they have tried to reduce the number of the entities. They say that it is logical simplicity as per the maxim धर्मिकल्पनापेक्षया धर्मकल्पना वरीयसी ! If the knowledge and behaviour can be well explained by the existent entities-one should not accept an additional one.

Select Bibliography

1. *Prakarṇapañcikā* Ed. by Subrahmanya Shastri, BHU, Varanasi.
2. *Abhāvavāda* of the *Tattvacintāmaṇi* of Ga ge'sa. Eng. Tr., B.K. Matilal, *HOS*, Harward University Press.
3. *Nañvāda* of Raghunāthat Śiromaṇi, Eng. Tr., B.K. Matilal, *Hos*, Harward University Press.
4. *Nyāyasiddhāntamuktāvali* of Viśvanātha, Chowkhamba Sanskrit Series, Varanasi.
5. *Mānameyodaya* of nārayaṇa, Adyur Library, Madras.
6. Śaktivāda of Gadādhara, Chowkhamba Sanskrit Series, Varanasi.
7. *Tarkasaṅgraha* of Annaṁbhaṭṭa, Athalye and Bodas, BORI, Poona.
8. *The Prābhākara School of Purvamīimāṁsā*, Ganganātha Jha, Delhi; Motilal Banarsidas.
9. *Doctrine of Negation*, B.K. Matilal, *HOS*, Harward University Press.

10

On Editing Murāri Miśra

Upto the third decade of this century very little was known about Murāri Miśra, the founder of the third school of *Pūrvamīmāṁsā. (PM)*. In this and the following decades some fragments of his work i.e. his commentary on *Jaiminisūtras* were published in the Journal of Oriental Research, Madras (*JORM*) and Annals of Bhandarkar Oriental Research Institute, Poona (ABORI). These *adhikaraṇas* are the only direct source to know his views on various important philosophical and logical concepts— as no other work of Murāri himself or any commentary on any of these fragments have seen the light of the day yet. There are not more manuscripts even to collate with. These facts make it very difficult to edit his text.

It is true that these texts are published but they could be treated as manuscripts so long as they are not understood thoroughly and then edited, if I may say so.

Out of the extant fragments mentioned above, I have confined myself to the *Arthavādādhikaraṇa* only for this paper, as I have attempted already to edit it. It is published from New Delhi, by Sri Satguru Publications.

The *Arthavādādhikaraṇa* was first edited by S.K. Ramanatha Shastri of Madras University and was published in *JORM* in 1928 (Vol. II, parts 3 and 4). Though he had edited it, it can be said that it was necessary to edit it further to obtain a coherent meaning out of it. While studying Murāri, I tried to do the same. In this paper I would like to show some of the examples which may demonstrate my claim. Nevertheless at some places I was benefitrded by the suggestions of S.K. Ramanatha Shastri.

Before we go to the examples, let us see in brief what is the content of this *adhikaraṇa* which will help us grasp the examples.

About the Content of the Adhikaraṇa

The aim of the *Arthavādādhikaraṇa* is to establish the validity of the *arthavāda* sentences which form an important part of the Veda. At the very outset, Murāri has stated the *pūrvapakṣa (Pp)* of Prābhākara, as attested in the *Bṛhatī*. The main objection of the *pūrvapakṣin (Pp)* is that *arthavādas* are merely narrative and since the Veda is meant for enjoining some action or the other, *arthavādas* cannot be treated as valid so long as their *kriyārthatva* is not proved. These sentences being narrative cannot form sentence-unity with the injunctions as well, hence they are not authoritative.

The *siddhānta* of Prābhākara also is repeated by Murāri thereafter. In nutshell it is as follows : since the *Adhyayanavidhi* enjoins the study of the whole Veda, in order to maintain the authority of this *vidhi* the *arthavādas* have to be authoritative. For that they must form the sentence-unity with the *vidhis* even by changing their forms. *Vidhis* also require the praise to induce a person to take up an activity

Murāri does not agree with this line of thought of the *Pp*. and also that of the *Siddhānta*. According to him *Pp*. must be formed on the basis of sentence-unity itself. Because, then only the *pūrvapaksin* will be able to challenge the main proposition of the previous *pāda* and then alone the consistency in the argument could be maintained.

Murāri, discussing various important concepts like that of sentence-unity, *kārya* and *siddha*, *viśeṣaṇa* and *upalakṣaṇa* elaborates how the sentence-unity between the *vidhis* and the *arthavādas* can be achieved. Main portion of this *adhikarana* discusses this very issue.

In the *Arthavādādhikaraṇa* of the *Śābarabhāṣya*, Śabarasvāmin has discussed the issue with some examples of *arthavāda* sentences such as : *Rudraḥ kila ruroda yadarodīt tadrudrasya rudratvam* or *Vāyur vai kṣepiṣṭhā devatā/vāyum eva svena bhāgadheyena upadhāvati, sa eva enam bhūtim gamayati* etc. As they are well known by very frequent occurrences in almost all the texts of *PM* Murāri does not quote them himself. Nevertheless, he speaks about them taking for granted that all are aware of these examples.

About the Text

With this background, let us now discuss some of the places where the text needs some revision.

(1 While defining the concepts of *kārya* and *siddha* Murāri states : कृत्यनुरञ्जनयोग्यं कार्यमत्र अभिप्रेतम्। तच्च द्वयम्–नियोज्यकोटि: विषयकोटिश्च। कोटिद्वयबहिर्भूतं सिद्धमभिप्रेतम्।

Tr : That which is fit to be associated with the volition (*kṛti*) is what is meant by *kārya* here. That will fall under the category of either *niyojya* or under the category of *viṣaya* (of *kṛti*). And that which falls outside the domain of these two is intended (to be known) as *siddha*

And says further : न चातीतस्य च ओदनादेर्वर्तमानस्य च वायुक्षेपिष्ठत्वादे: कोटिद्वये यीग्यता विद्यते इति नैकवाक्यत्वम्। इति।

Tr. Neither the rice which occurred in the past nor the present fastness or swiftness of the deity *vāyu* is fit to be included in either of these two categories (of *kārya*) and therefore, there cannot be the sentence-unity (of the *arthavādas* and the injunctions.)

One will not fail to see here that the word *odana* is a misfit in this expression, as there is no context of *odana* here. Because it is not only past but it can as well be present and also future.

As the two sentences i.e. *Rudrah kila ruroda* and *vāyur vai kṣepiṣtha devatā* occur together in many texts on *PM* right from the *Bhāṣya* of *Śabara* one feels sure that the word *Odana* has occurred here in place of *rodana* by mistake. And it goes without saying that this *rodana* (i.e. weeping) refers to the *Rudrarodana* only. Because it occurred as per the story in the Veda in the past only so it can be referred to as *atitarodana*.

And hence I have corrected this sentence as : न चातीतस्य च रोदनादेर्वर्तमानस्य च वायुक्षेपिष्ठत्वादे: कोटिद्वये योग्यता विद्यते इति नैकवाक्यत्वम्। (vide A reconstruction of the Third School of *PM*, Sri Garibdas Oriental Series No. 90, Sri Satguru Publications, New Delhi, 1990, p. 115).

(2) Now look at this : यद्यप्येकवाक्यता न प्रतीयते; तथाप्यध्ययन–विधिना सर्वस्य वेदस्य प्रयोजनवदर्थपरत्वापादानादर्थवादानां तत्सिद्धयर्थं रूपभङ्गेनाप्येकवाक्यत्वं लक्षणयाङ्गीकर्तव्यं विधेरपि इतिकर्तव्यतात्वेन प्राशस्त्यस्यापेक्षणादिति।

Here I have changed the word *prayojanavadarthapartvāpādānād* to *prayojanavadarthaparatvāpādanāt* to make the sentence meaningful as word *āpādāna* does not carry any meaning (vide ibid, p. 115).

(3) In another place the opponent has raised the following doubt :

नन्वेकवाक्यतयापि कथं पूर्वपक्षः? सा हि क्रियाकारकादिपदेषु विभक्त्यादिबलात् भवति। विभक्त्या संनिहितपदार्थप्रतियोगिककारणत्वस्याभिधानात्। इह तु द्वयोरनुपहताख्यातयोः न व्युत्पत्तिसिद्धा एकवाक्यता। वाक्यभेद एव तु व्युत्पन्नः।

(vide ibid, p. 147)

Tr : Well, (our basic doubt is) how can there be the *pūrvapakṣa* framed on the basis of sentence-unity (of *vidhis* and *arthavādas*)? Because such sentence-unity is possible on the basis of case terminations and personal suffixes occurring in inflected forms expressive of action and the *kārakas* because the suffixes express the relation of causality, the counter correlative of which is the meaning of a word adjacent to the suffix. Whereas here, the two sentences have two verbal forms neither of which is subordinated and so there cannot be normal sentence-unity here. On the contrary, they clearly are two independent sentences.

To answer this Murāri points out :

उच्यते–सिद्धसिद्धार्थसाध्यार्थान्वययोरप्याख्यतयोः एकवाक्यत्वं व्युत्पन्नम्। हेतुहेतुमद्भावेन चान्वयः। यथा मलिनं ते वपुः वर्तते, स्नायाः।

Here as one can see one *'siddha'* in the beginning of the sentence is superfluous. Hence I have deleted it in my edition of the work (vide ibid, p. 148). This gives us a coherent meaning that the sentence unity is possible between two sentences having two separate verbal forms one denoting the relation with the already accomplished thing and the other denoting the relation with something yet to be accomplished. Such a relation between the two (sentences) can be that of probans and probandum relationship as in the case, for instance, your body is dirty, you should take bath, etc.

(4) Now look at this :

ननुक्तमुपलक्षणं अन्यव्यवच्छेदकं न भवति। यथाकमण्डलुना च्छात्रमानय इति च्छात्रान्तरं व्यवच्छिद्यते। न चात्र तदस्ति, अप्रशस्तस्य वायोर्व्यवच्छिद्यमानस्य अभावात्।

Here, looking at the context one feels that the negative

particle in the first sentence has to be dropped here. I have done the same thing, which results into the following meaning : Well, *upalakṣaṇa* is a differentiator of something from something else. For instance when someone says, Bring the student having the pitcher (the pitcher) distinguishes that student from the other students. But here, such is not the case, because there is no *vāyu* which is not praised and which could be distinguished thereby.

(vide ibid p. 184).

If we accept the text as it is printed will give us exactly the opposite meaning which does not suit the context.

(5) We have seen before that Murāri has discussed elaborately how the sentence-unity between the *vidhis* and the *arthavādas* can be achieved.

In this discussion the opponent raises some doubts about the issue. One doubt is that there is no expectancy on the part of the injunctive sentence and hence *prāśastya* or the meaning of the *arthavādas* cannot be connected with them. As this doubt is answered another question is raised by the opponent as follows :

न च–लाक्षणिकत्वादनुवादानां नाभिधानापर्यवसानम् अतश्च कथमाकाङ्क्षा-इति वाच्यम् ।

Tr : One should not argue that since the *anuvādas* are *lākṣaṇika*, they do result into expressing their primary sense and thus how can there be any expectancy (for the *anuvādas* on the part of the *vidhis*)?

I have amended the text here from नाभिधानापर्यवसानं to नाभिधानपर्यवसानं which gives us the consistent meaning namely : one should not argue that since the *anuvādas* denote their secondary meaning they do not result into expressing their primary sense and thus how can there be any expectancy?

(vide ibid, p. 187).

If the text is accepted as it is printed it gives us the meaning first shown in the tr. above, which does not make any consistent argument, but sounds contradictory.

(6) Now look at this : यतः सर्वलक्षणासाधारणत्वात् । तस्मादभिधान-ग्रहणम् उपलक्षणं तत्र, तात्पर्यापर्यवसानं तु तत्र विवक्षितम् ।

Tr : Because this phenomenon is common to all cases of *lakṣaṇā*. Therefore, the understanding of their primary meaning is only an indicator (to the secondary meaning and) what is intended to be understood from them is only not the intention of the speaker.

Here also, as one can see, one negative particle is an extra element. Hence I have changed the expression from तात्पर्यपर्यवसानं तु ....to तात्पर्यपर्यवसानं तु ..... which gives us the better reading and so better understanding of the text, as then it means : .....Therefore, the understanding.... (...and) what is intended to be understood from them is only the intention of the speaker (vide ibid, p. 188).

(7) Following the same line the text reads : यद्याकाङ्क्षाकल्पने न अन्विताभिधानम् उभयाकाङ्क्षालक्षणत्वात् सम्बन्धस्य.... अतः कथं तदविवक्षितमिति चेत्....,

If we try to translate this as it is it will be something like this : If someone argues here that if you do not connect (the *vidhis* and the *arthavādas*) on the strength of the postulation of expectancy because expectancy on the part of both sides is the definition of a relation then... And then how is it said that it (the expectancy) is not intended there (to be postulated)?

After translating this one feels sure that this could not be the proper way of argument. If we simply connect (यद्याकाङ्क्षाकल्पने न अन्विता .... etc. into one single word then the reading will be.... (यद्याकाङ्क्षाकल्पनेनान्विता ..... And then the sentence will mean : If someone argues here that if you connect (the *vidhis* and the *arthavādas*) on the strength of the postulation of expectancy because expectancy on the part of both sides is the definition of relation then....etc. This sounds to be logical and hence this is how I have accepted the reading of this text (vide ibid, p.188).

Obsertions

These are some examples where the text of *Arthavādādhikaraṇa* of M.M. Murāri Miśra needed some revision and amendations. There are two or three more which I have not mentioned here. First obvious problem in editing the text of Murāri is that there is only one *Ms*. This does not enable us to collate it with others to find a better reading. Another one is that there is no commentary on his text available to us today. This also would have been a source of help while deciding the readings. Nor is there any rich tradition of his followers which would have quoted Murāri every now and then. It is true that we have many references to Murāri's doctrine in the philosophical texts on Nyāya and Mīmāṁsā but in all these texts he appears as a *Pp.* who is refuted by them. None of these texts have quoted the *Arthavādādhikaraṇa*.

In such a situation the only way left is to decide a reading on the basis of the understanding of internal logic, basic tenets of the system the context in which the word occurs and so on.

I have discussed so far what actually were the difficulties in understanding the text of M.M. Murāri Miśra and how I have solved them. I do not claim that my interpretation is the final one. If a better reading is suggested by somebody which offers a better understanding of the text, my reading may be revised.

Also if some more manuscripts of the same work of Murāri are found or some commentary on him is found or if some other work of Murāri comes into light, we shall be in a better position to interpret the text before us.

I have already hinted that this is a case where no other source of help is there either in the form of more *mss* or in that of some commentary etc. I, therefore, think that so long as these are not available, these readings suggested by me could be treated as possible interpretations. Scholars are the best judges here.

11

Murāri Miśra on Kārya and Siddha

Concept of *Kārya* is much discussed a concept in the system of *Pūrvamīmāṁsā (PM)* because it is an important postulation of the 'Intermediate Causal Link' (*apūrva*) between the performance of sacrifice and its result namely heaven etc. It has also another meaning which is common to the classical Sanskrit Language i.e. something to be done or to be achieved. Actually, this is the primary meaning of the word which is extended by the *Mīmāṁsakas* to the meaning of apūrva mentioned above.

In this paper, I have discussed the definitions of *kārya* and *siddha* as given by Murāri Miśra, the exponent of the Third School of *PM*. I have also tried to analyse the definitions and point out how Murāri differs from the *Prābhākaras*.

The context in which Murāri speaks about the concepts of *kārya* and *siddha* is that of establishing the validity of the *arthavāda*—sentences of the Veda. The *Jaiminisūtra* 1.2.1 states that, that part of the Veda which does not enjoin any activity is not valid because the whole Veda is meant for prompting men into some action, some performance.

(आम्नायस्य क्रियार्थत्वादानर्थक्यमतदर्थक्यमतदर्थानाम् । JS. 1.2.1)

According to this rule the position of the *arthavādas* becomes doubtful as they are nothing more than narrative sentences. They sentences like Vāyu is the swiftest deity or he cried etc. (i.e. वायुर्वे क्षेपिष्ठा देवता or सोऽरोदीत्) have nothing to do with any activity. They either narrate some facts or tell some stories of the Past. And hence these sentences cannot be considered, as they are, as valid as per the rule stated above. But there is a way of making them valid and that is to unite them with the injunctive sentences. Because if they are connected with the injunctions, they can be treated as expressive of *kārya* or action. To explain, if a particular *arthavāda* is connected with a particular injunction then it becomes just a part of the injunctive sentence and one sentence expresses only one coherent meaning according to the *Mīmāṁsakas*. Thus, the *arthavada* united with an injunction will express the same action as expressed by that injunction and thence be valid with reference to *Dharma*.

Anticipating this possibility, the opponent of Prābhākara begins with an argument which rules out this very possibility Murāri has quoted the *pūrvapakṣa* of Prābhākara in the very beginning of his *Arthavādāhikaraṇa* of the *Tripādīnītinayana*. The argument of the opponent of Prābhākara, as stated by Murāri is that *arthavādas* cannot be treated as expressive of *kārya* because there is no ground to connect them with the injunctions. It is implied here that if they are so connected they will express the same meaning as that of the injunctions and will be valid so far as Dharma is concerned.

Murāri, at the very outset rejects this formation of the *pūrvapakṣa*. According to him, instead of arguing in this way, one should rather state it this way : It is not possible to argue on the side of the validity of the *arthavādas* with reference to *Dharma* because they are expressive of *siddhārtha* i.e. they express the meanings which are already accomplished that do not prompt men into any action. Further, one should consider the question : why sentence-unity between the *arthavādas* and the injunctions is not possible? The answer to this question would be, only *kārya* meaning can be related to another *kārya* meaning. And the *arthavādas* do not convey *kārya*-meanings.

On this the opponent is reminded of the case of *niyojya*. *Niyojya* is that person who is prompted to take up an action (vide : 'नियोज्यस्स च कार्यं यः स्वकीयत्वेन बुध्यते' वाक्यार्थमातृका of प्रकरणपञ्चिका)

The person obviously cannot be treated as *kāryārtha* or *sādhāyrtha*. He is no doubt a *siddhārtha*. Then, the opponent asks, how is it that the *niyojya* being *siddha* is construed with the meaning of the injunction which is *kārya*? Here is the case of *siddhartha* being connected with a meaning which is not *siddha*. If this is allowed then there should be no difficulty in connecting the meaning of the *arthavadas* with the meaning of the injunctions. Not only this but there are also some more cases like that of the Time etc. which are also *siddha* and in spite of this fact are connected with the *kārya* or meaning which is yet to be achieved or established i.e. the action. If one argues here that because of their (of *kāla* etc.) association with the action they become *sādhya* then this will lead to the fault of mutual dependency : If there is association with the action (the *siddha* entities) become *sādhya* and if they are *sādhya* they can be associated with the action. To quote Murāri :

क्रियान्वये साध्यता साध्यत्वे च क्रियान्वय इति दुरुत्तरमितरेतराश्रयं स्यात् ।
(vide : *A Reconstruction of the Third School of PM.* by Ujjwala Panse, Sri Satguru Publications New Delhi, 1990, p. 113)

To avoid this fault of mutual dependency, Murāri argues, we should define the concepts of *kārya* and *siddha* and also their scope. It is here that Murāri has defined these two concepts. He says :

तस्मादेवं वाच्यम्-कृत्यनुरञ्जनयोग्यं कार्यमत्र अभिप्रेतम्। तच्च द्वयम्-नियोज्यकोटिः विषयकोटिश्च। कोटिद्वयबहिर्भूतं सिद्धमभिप्रेतम्।

(vide ibid, p. 113)

In this context, *kārya* is that which is fit to be associated with an action. This again should be divided into two groups, namely, the group of *niyojya* and the group of *viṣaya*. To explain : one group of *kārya* will be the group of the person who is prompted to take up an activity and the other will be that of the object of performance namely *yāga* or sacrifice. Whatever falls outside the domain of these two is to be considered as *siddha*.

In other words Murāri intends to say that *kārya* consists of two heads (1) *Niyojya* i.e. the performer or the person to take up the action and (2) the sacrifice itself. Nothing more nothing less. Whatever is not covered by these two heads is not fit to be called *kārya* but it should be named as *siddha*.

The meanings conveyed by the *arthavādas* like, सोऽरोदीत् or वायुर्वै क्षेपिष्ठा देवता etc. obviously, do not fall under these two and hence cannot be called *kārya*. Thus, that which is not fit to be included in these two groups cannot be called *kārya* and in turn cannot be connected with the injunction or the meaning of injunctive sentence e.g. 'the weeping of Rudra' or 'swiftness of the deity *vāyu*'. being past and present respectively cannot form either of these two groups and hence are *siddha* and not *kārya*. Therefore, they cannot be united with the injunctive sentences.

Murāri has pointed out here the way of forming an appropriate *pūrvapakṣa*. He has defined these two concepts in this particular context. Because he wants to avoid the ambiguity. By defining *kārya* the way he has done it, he has included the *siddha niyojya* in the category of *kārya* and has brought it to the level where it is connected with the sacrifice which is *kārya* without any difficulty.

Observations

From the way Murāri has defined *kārya* it is clear, in my opinion, that whatever is *kriyārtha* i.e. meant for an action is *kārya* for him, of course, besides the action itself. The *JS* 1.2.1 states that only that part of the Veda is valid which is meant for some action or the other and whatever does not help the action in any way to come into the being is not valid because the Veda as a whole is meant for prompting man into an action. This implies that which is already an accomplished entity cannot be considered as valid in the context of *Dharma* unless and until it is associated with an action. I think what is meant by the word *kriyārtha* in *JS*. 1.2.1 corresponds to Murāri's idea of *kārya*. To make it clear, look how Murāri has defined it. He says *kṛtyanurañjanayogya* is *kārya* i.e. which is fit to be related with an action. In other words, *kārya* is that which will help the action to come into existence in some way or the other. By defining it this way what could he achieve? It is this : As per the primary or say conventional meaning of *kārya* we cannot include any already established entity in the sphere of it because it that way corresponds to the concept of *sādhya* as it were. Thus we cannot think of any *siddha* entity becoming *kārya* i.e. *sādhya* as per the primary meanings of both. But by defining the concepts the way he has done it, Murāri can include the *niyojya* i.e. the performer of the sacrifice into the domain of *kārya* entities. Performer actually brings about the action and he is truly indispensable so far as any performance of sacrifice is concerned. But as per the rule *kārya* alone can be related with *kārya* there is no way to connect the performer with the action if the primary meanings of *kārya* and *siddha* are taken into account, and thus, he will remain unconnected with the action which in no way is desirable. But Murāri's definition of *kārya* includes *niyojya* also in the realm of *kārya* and solves the problem. Thus, the purpose of the definition is clear from the context in which Murāri has defined kārya.

If we compare Murāri's concept of *kārya* with that of *Prābhākaras'* then it becomes evident that Murāri's concept is wider than *Prābhākaras'*. To elaborate : *Prābhākaras* have also defined *kārya* as

कृतसम्बन्धि हि कार्यम्

(vide *Tantrarahasya*, p.46) i.e. they also intend that which is related with the *kṛti* is *kārya* but here the term 'related' 'or' 'सम्बधि' is used in a restricted sense. To my mind the meaning of 'related' is 'produced by' i.e. to say that which is produced by *kṛti* is *kārya* and not merely related in any way so to say. Śālikanātha has expressedly said that *kārya* is *kṛtisādhya* (vide *Prakaraṇapañcikā, vākyārthanātṛkā*, verse 7). Thus, this definition of *kārya* will not allow *niyojya* to become *kārya* in any way. Rather Śālikanātha has defined it in the *Prakaraṇapañcikā* as follows : It is different from the sacrifice, exists at different time than the sacrifice and is fit to be related with *niyojya* (vide *vākyārthamātṛkā*, verse 23). Obviously what *Prābhākaras* have in mind is *apūrva* which is produced by the sacrifice and nothing else.

Thus, it is clear from whatever we have discussed so far that as per that definition of Murāri we can include *Prābhākaras' kārya* i.e. *apūrva* under the concept of *kārya* as it is fit to be related with *kṛti* by *janya-janaka-bhāva* relation as well as we can bring *niyojya, kāla* etc. also under the domain of *kārya*. Because Murāri has stated the relation in general and not any particular relation. *Apūrva* can very well be included in the *viṣayakoṭi* of *kārya* as it will form the object of sacrifice and also of *kṛti*.

References

1. *Mīmāṁsā Darśana* with *Śābarabhāṣya* and *Tantravārtika*, Anandashram Sanskrit Granthāvali, No.97, Pune, 1970.
2. *Prakaraṇapañcikā* with *Nyāyasiddhi*, B.H.U., Darsana Series-4, B.H.U. Publication, 1961.
3. *Tantrarahasya* of Rāmānuja, Oriental Institute, Baroda, 1956.
4. A reconstruction of the Third School of *Pūrvamīmāṁsā*. Sri Garibdass Oriental Series 90 Sri Satguru Publications, 1990.

12

Murāri Miśra on Tantra and Āvāpa

Tantra and *āvāpa* are important concepts in *pūrvamīmāṁsā* as they are directly involved in deciding the scope of the performance of a particular subsidiary rite. These two concepts are discussed by Śabara in the 11th chapter of his *bhāṣya*. He has commented upon the concept of *tantra* elaborately. *Āvāpa* is not however discussed at length. It seems that this concept is somewhat simpler than *tantra*.

तत्र यत्सकृत्कृतं बहूनामुपकरोति तत्तन्त्रमित्युच्यते। यथा बहूनां ब्राह्मणानां मध्ये कृतः प्रदीपः। यस्त्वावृत्त्योपकरेति स आवापः। यथा तेषामेव ब्राह्मणानामनुलेपनम्।

(*ŚBH* on *JS* 11.1.1)

Tr : That which performed once helps many is what is called *tantra*, just as a lamp lit among many Brahmins (gives light to all of them) (And) that which helps by repeated performance is called *āvāpa*, just as anointing of the same Brahmins (each *Brāhmaṇa* has to be anointed separately.)

Ritualistic example of *tantra* is that of अग्न्याधान. The fire once placed ceremonially i.e. as per the prescribed injunctions helps the offerings of many oblations alike—Śabara explains. He also said elsewhere in the *ŚBh*. : तन्त्रंनाम साधारणो धर्मग्रामः। स येषां प्रधानानां तानि तन्त्रीणि प्रधानानि। which also helps us understand what तन्त्र is.

The concept of *āvāpa* is less controversial or we may say less complicated. There is no complication because the performance takes place as many times the rite is enjoined. Hence there is no question of defining the area or scope of application of this concept.

But such is not the case with *tantra*. There is another concept namely *prasaṅga* which is similar to the concept of *tantra* and thence makes it somewhat difficult, as it were, to decide whether a particular performance in particular situation helps many being *tantra* or whether it is a case of *prasaṅga*. Because प्रसङ्ग also helps more than one be it undesirable. To understand it properly, let us see in brief, what is *prasaṅga*. Śabara has defined *prasaṅga* as follows :

अन्यत्र कृतस्य अन्यत्रापि प्रसक्तिः प्रसङ्गः । यथा प्रदीपस्य प्रासादे कृतस्य राजमार्गेऽपि आलोककरणम् । (*ŚBh*. on *J.S.* 12.1.1).

Tr : That which is performed for something else extends somewhere else for which it is not meant. The example is sufficient to make it clear : As a lamp kindled in the palace of a king also illumines the highway before the king's palace.

It is clear that the lamp in the example is not meant for illuminating the street but it does so without any additional effort. If we compare the example of *tantra* with this one, the difference between the two becomes obvious. The lamp kindled among many *Brāhmaṇas* was meant for them when it was kindled. In other words, the agent knew that his act was going to oblige more than one and knowingly he performed the act with an intention of helping many thereby. But the lamp in the example of *prasaṅga* is meant only for the illumination of the palace and not of the street. nevertheless it illumines the street, all the same. Here the agent does not intend or expect to illumine the street, i.e. he does not intend that the act taken up by him should oblige more than one but still this is what actually happens.

Since both the cases have a meagre degree of difference, there is a chance that one takes or rather mistakes one for another. And this is the reason perhaps why the concept of *tantra* is discussed at length by Śabara in the 11th chapter of his *bhāṣya* and by Murāri in his monograph entitled, '*Ekādaśādyādhikaraṇa*'.

We have seen how Śabara has explained the difference between the two concepts and how he has defined *āvāpa*. Now let us see what Murāri has to say on the concepts of *tantra* and *āvāpa*.

When we come to the *Ekādaśādyādhikaraṇa* of Murāri we find that he begins by quoting the first *sūtra* of *Jaiminisūtras* of the first *adhikaraṇa* of the 11th chapter, and takes up the concept of *tantra* at first, for discussion.

He has clearly stated in this text that *āvāpa* is a general rule because it is nothing but the performance as many times as it is enjoined. Hence there is no question or doubt about its nature. Therefore the subject matter of the chapter is *tantra* i.e. the chapter aims at discussing the concept of *tantra* and not that of *āvāpa*.

To quote Murāri, आवापस्तु यथाप्रप्तिभेदेनानुष्ठानम् इति सुव्यक्तमेव। तन्त्रमेवाध्यायार्थो नावापः । प्राप्तिभेदेनावापस्य औत्सर्गिकत्वेनाजिज्ञासितत्वात् । (एकादशाद्याधिकरण; आवापस्वरुपविमर्शः)

The first line mentioned above is the definition of *āvāpa* given by Murāri. He has also given another definition of *āvāpa* in the *adhikarana* which runs as follows: अनेकार्थस्यानेकमनुष्ठानम् अनेकार्थम् आवापः । Which means, many performances, subsidiary to many and meant for many is what is called *āvāpa*. But he does not discuss the concept of *āvāpa* more anywhere of these two places, the reason of which he has stated himself (ibid).

By saying that *tantra* is the object of discussion of the 11th chapter Murāri has expressed his view that it is more complicated a concept which needs to be discussed at length.

He has taken into account some of the possible definitions of *tantra* and has discarded all of them on some ground or the other and has offered a definition which he thinks is a proper definition of *tantra*.

Some of the definitions that he has refuted are in order :

यदि सकृत्त्वमेव तन्त्रत्वं तदा सोमे दीक्षणीयादीनां तन्त्रत्वं स्यात् ।

If तन्त्रत्व is defined as oneness then even the दीक्षणीयेष्टि in the *soma* sacrifice will have to be treated as *tantra*. Because it is performed once in the sacrifice and hence possesses oneness namely *tantratva*. This definition, thus suffers from the fault of over-application. He then takes up another definition :

अथानेकोपकारकत्वे सत्येकत्वं तर्हि प्रसङ्गेऽपि तन्त्रत्वप्रसङ्गः ।

If we define it as being one, subsidiary to many or helping many then this definition will over apply to the concept of *prasaṅga*.

One more definition refuted by Murāri is, अनेकशेषत्वे सति एकम् अनेकोपकारकं तन्त्रम् । *Tantra* is that which is subsidiary of many and being one helps many. Then this definition will not apply to the *purodāśakapālas* i.e. it suffers from the fault of *avyāpti* or narrow application. Murāri concludes this phase of discussion by saying that *tantra* cannot also be defined as 'the absence of repetition' but it should be defined as 'one performance which is meant for all'. To quote Murāri : नावृत्त्यभाव: तन्त्रत्वं किन्त्वेकस्यानुष्ठानस्य सर्वार्थत्वम् । (ibid)

Once we define *tantra* in this way it means that if one performance is meant for all then since there remains no purpose to be served by another performance, the act is not performed again. But the point to be noted is that this absence of second performance is not what is called *tantra* but the first performance which was meant for all should be designated as *tantra*. Murāri says : तथा च प्रयोजनाभावात् अनुष्ठानान्तरं न भवति । न तु सैव तन्त्रता । येन एव पदार्थस्यैकमनुष्ठानमनेकार्थं तन्त्रता । (ibid). It is clear from this statement of Murāri that he does not want to define the concept negatively but he insists that instead of defining it as an absence of something it should be defined in a positive manner so that one is able to know what consists of *tantra* or what is the referent of the term *tantra*.

Murāri has also quoted the definition of *tantra* given by Śabara and the comment that he has made thereon is significant. To quote Murāri.

अत्र भाष्यम्–तन्त्रं नाम "यत्सकृत्कृतं बहूनामुपकरोति" तदप्रयोज्ये प्रसङ्गे च गतमिति मत्वा टीकाकृता व्याख्यातम्–तन्त्रं नाम भेदेन प्राप्तौ सत्यां सकृदनुष्ठानेनार्थसिद्धि: । (ibid)

The *ŚBh* definition of *tantra* is overapplicable to *prasaṅga* and hence the commentator has explained it as, 'that which is enjoined separately (but) the purpose is served (merely) by its one performance' is called तन्त्र

We have to translate in this way according to Murāri. After quoting the above-stated comment of the *tīkākṛt*, Murāri explains that the obtainment of the purpose cannot be treated as *tantra* because it will go against the *ŚBh* if we accept such a view, but the subsidiaries of the main sacrifice or main *apūrva* to be produced by the sacrifice are named as *tantra*.

Observations

To conclude, from whatever we have discussed so far, we feel that Murāri has contributed to the system of *Pūrvamīmāṁsā* in various ways : (1) Murāri has maintained his distinguishedness by commenting on the concept of *tantra* so elaborately which is not done by Kumārila. The *Tupṭīkā* on the 1st *adhikaraṇa* of the 11th chapter of the *ŚBh* is very short whereas Murāri has written a separate *adhikaraṇa* on it. We are not in a position to say anything for certain about Prabhākara as Bṛhatī on that part of *ŚBh*. is not available to us today. But so far as Kumārila is concerned Murāri has shown his difference clearly. (2) Murāri's style does not match exactly with that of Śabara. Śabara has given many examples of *tantra* for clarifying the concept, whereas Murāri has discussed various definitions of *tantra* and by showing the faults of over application or narrow application in certain cases has refuted them all, and has presented a definition which he thinks proper. In this way, he has contributed to clarify the concept by defining it precisely. We can see that he has been influenced by the style of *Navya Nyāya*— which also aimed at disambiguating the concepts by defining them as precisely as possible. (3) His one more contribution is of a different type and that is the quotation of the comment of a *tīkākṛt*. This *ṭīkākṛt* seems to be none else than the great *Guru* or Prabhākara. The same line is quoted by Candra, follower of Prabhākara School of *PM* in this *Nyāyaratnākara* under the name of the *Guru*. Thus, even if the *Bṛhatī* or *Laghvī* for that matter are not available on the 11th chapter of the *ŚBh*, we could have an access to the opinion of Prabhākara only because of Murāri and the other writer mentioned above. (4) The quotation is aptly stated for removing the defect in the *ŚBh* definition of *tantra*. The quoting of the comment of the *ṭīkākṛt* is worthy of mention because otherwise the definition offered by Śabara really suffers from the fault of over application. In case of प्रसङ्ग it is not the case that there is separate injunction which enjoins its separate performance but the purpose is served automatically by one performance. No. But this is exactly the situation in case of *tantra*. And this is the actual difference between the two. To understand the difference between these two concepts the comment of the टीकाकृत् is very much helpful. That is why I said that Murāri has quoted him aptly.

Thus, to conclude, I repeat the saying :

"मुरारेः तृतीयः पन्थाः ।"

References

1. *Mīmāṁsā Darśan* of Jaimini, Anandashram Sanskrit Granthavali, No. 97, Vol. 7, Pune, 1974.
2. *Śābarabhāṣya* of Śabaraswamin, Anandashram Sanskrit Granthavali, No. 97, Vol. 7, Pune, 1974.
3. *Tupṭīkā* of Kumārila Bhaṭṭa, Anandashram Sanskrit Granthavali, No. 97, Vol. 7, Pune, 1974.
4. *Nyāyaratnākara* of Candra.
5. *Ekādaśādyādhikaraṇa* of Murāri Miśra, Published in Annals of the Bhandarkar Oriental Research Institute, Pune, 1929.
6. *A Reconstruction of the Third School of Pūrvamīmāṁsā* by Ujjwala Panse, Sri Garibdass Oriental Series, No. 90, Sri Satguru Publications, New Delhi, 1990

13

Omens : Past and Present

Man has always been curious about the things or happenings which are beyond the range of his perception. He likes to know his own future which is yet to come. The desire to see the unseen future right at present time has led him to search for the means of knowing it if any at all. Apparently this search has been fruitful and the fruit takes the form either of augury or divination or omens or fortune-telling or the totems and manitou etc. Though all of these are mostly interrelated and operate in very similar ways, we, here, are specifically concerned with the 'omens'.

The concept is not unfamiliar in any part of the world. The movements of birds or beasts are considered ominous in some degree by nearly if not quite all races (vide : Encyclopaedia of Religion and Ethics, Ed. James Hastings, 1911 Vol. iv, pp. 775). it is a matter of dispute in many civilized communities whether any validity can be attributed to the concept and it is mostly beyond dispute in the rational community that the concept is fallacious. But then there are people who accept it as valid and act or react accordingly.

For the time being let us keep aside the question of validity and relevance of the concept and try to look into some of the oldest references to the concept in Sanskrit literature which may help us find the ancient Indian sources of it.

Sanskrit word for omen is *Śakuna*. *Śakuna* primarily means a bird. It seems to me that basically the word meant only a bird and since a bird played very significant role as an indicator of future happenings either good or bad, the same word denoted the meaning 'omen' secondarily. At present it is a polysemous word denoting both a bird as well as an omen. There is another similar word which also stands both for a bird and for an omen. This helps strengthen our above hypothesis. That word is *Śakunī*. *Śakunī* also primarily meant a bird but later on it is more popularly used in the sense of an omen (vide : *Vaidikakośa* by Suryakant, Benares Hindu University, 1963, p. 502).

There are ample references which show that cries of birds or birds themselves were believed to indicate forthcoming good or evil happenings—right from the time of the *Rg Veda*. The following lines bear the proof of it.

References to Śakuna found in Ancient Indian Literature

The oldest verbal testimony namely the *Ṛg Veda (Ṛv)* contains many verses which mention some birds as indicating good or evil happenings in future. *Ṛv.* 2.42 and *Ṛv.* 2.43 are named *Śakunasūktas* where *śakuna* means simply a bird. According to Sāyaṇa the bird referred to here is *kapiñjala*. Both the hymns are addressed to this bird. The seer prays :

कनिक्रदज्जनुषं प्रब्रुवाण इयर्ति वाचमरितेव नावम् ।
सुमङ्गलश्च शकुने भवासि मा त्वा का चिदभिभा
विश्व्या विदत् ।। 1 ।।
मा त्वा श्येन उद्वधीन्मा सुपर्णो मा त्वा
विददिषुमान्वीरो अस्ता ।
... अव क्रन्द दक्षिणतो गृहाणां सुमङ्गलो भद्रवादी शकुन्ते ।। *Ṛv.* 2.42

and also that

भद्रमा वद विश्वतो नः शकुने पुण्यमा वद ।
आवदस्त्वं शकुने भद्रमा वद तूष्णीमासीनः सुमतिं चिकिद्धि नः ।।
Ṛv. 2.43

Meaning : The bird frequently cries and proclaims the future and it propels its speech as an oarsman propels a boat. O bird, may you be auspicious to us, may no over-powering phenomenon reach you from any side. Let not the *śyena* (hawk) or *suparṇa* (some big bird) kill or harm you. Be talking auspicious things to us from all sides and when you are silent think good about us.

From this it may be observed that the bird to whom these hymns are addressed is an omen indicating good events in future and so the seer prays that this bird must not be harmed by the evil birds like *śyena* and *suparṇa*.

Suryakant in his *Vaidikakośa* opines that this bird indicates evil happening or bad luck. I do not agree with this for the reason just mentioned.

Kapiñjala is not directly referred to in the *Rg Veda* but if we accept Sāyaṇa then the hymns 2.42 and 2.43 are addressed to this particular bird. In my opinion, this is the same bird which is now-a-days known by the name *Bhāradvāja* in Marāthi. With this bird also the idea of good omen is attached today. There also is more proof to substantiate this hypothesis.

Maitrāyaṇī Saṁhitā (MS) gives the following story : Indra cut the three heads of the son of *Tvaṣṭā*. *Kapiñjala* was born from the head known as *somapa* : विश्वरूपो वै त्वाष्ट्र आसीत् त्रिशीर्षासुराणां स्वस्त्रीयः, स सोममेकेन शीर्ष्णापिबत् सुरामेकेना, अन्नमेकेनावयत् etc. तस्य यत् सोमपं शिरा आसीत् स कपिञ्जलोऽभवत् । (*MS*.2.4.1). In the *Śatapathabrāhmaṇa* (*ŚBr.*) also occurs the same story which also explains the origin of *kapiñjala*. One of the heads of the son of *tvaṣṭā* was known as *Somapāna* and from it was born the *kapiñjala*. Thus, it became hazel because the colour of *soma* is brownish. *ŚBr*. 1.6.3.3 runs as follows: स यत् सोमपानं (विश्वरूपस्य मुखम्) आस ततः कपिञ्जलः समभवत् स बभ्रुक इव बभ्रुरिव हि सोमो राजा । *Nirukta* 3.4.1 explains the etymology of the words as follows : कपिञ्जल कपिरिव जीर्णः कपिरिव जवते, ईषत् पिङ्गलो वा । *Kapiñjala* is that who is old like a monkey, or moves like a monkey or who is partly hazel in colour.

All this may lead us to conclude that the *kapiñjala* of older times is same as *Bhāradvāja* of modern times. To explain, the word *Bhāradvāja* in Marathi denotes a bird which is all black and its two wings only are *piṅgala* or brownish in colour. Thus, it is *Īsaptpiṅgala*. Not only this but its movement (i.e. jumping in the branches of trees) does resemble that of a monkey as mentioned by Yāska (*Nirukta* 3.4.1).

Ṛv. 10.165 contains several verses about a *kapota* bird and one about an owl :

देवाः कपोत इषितो यदिच्छन्दूतो निर्ऋत्या इदमाजगाम। तस्मा अर्चाम कृणवाम निष्कृतिं शं नो अस्तु द्विपदे शं चतुष्पदे ।। (*Ṛv*. 10.165.1)

also

यदुलूको वदति मोघमेतद् ....etc. *Ṛv*. 10.165.4.

Meaning - A *kapota* bird, Messenger of ill luck (*Nirṛti*) has come to our house, with whatever (evil) intent, we worship you, we shall perform atonement. O god, may it farewell with our men and quadrupeds. May what the owl expresses (by its hooting) turn out to be fruitless or untrue.

Aśvalāyanagṛhyasūtra (Aśv.gr.) prescribes the recitation of *Rv.* 2.42 and 43 along with some ritual if the unfavourable sound of birds is heard (वयसाममनोज्ञा वाचः श्रुत्वा कनिक्रदज्जनुषं प्रब्रुवाण इति सुक्ते जपेत् *Aśv. gṛ.* 3.10.9).

Taittirīya Samhitā (TS) refers to a black bird who brings about the death of the slaves of the *yajamāna*. यत्कृष्णशकुनः पृषदाज्यमवमृशेच्छूद्रा अस्य प्रमायुकाः स्यु etc. *TS* 3.2.6.2). This black bird might be crow as crow or cawing of crows is considered to be indicating coming evil in other places also.

Kauṣītakigṛhyasūtra (Kau. gṛ.) refers to *kākaśabda* as a bad omen and prescribes an expiation for it. (स्वप्नदर्शने निशायाम् । काकशब्दक्रान्ते च । अन्येषु चाद्भुतेषु च । पयसा चरुं श्रपयित्वा.... etc. *Kau. gṛ.* 5.5)

Ṣadviṁśa Brāhmaṇa (Ṣad Br.) 6.8.2 records perceiving a *kakamithuna* as a bad omen along with many others and adds that expiatory rites should be performed in such circumstances. Entering of *kāka* or *śyena* or *gṛdhra* into a residence is also an evil omen which needs some *prāyaścitta* rite to be performed.

Similarly, *Atharva Veda (Av)* contains many references to *Śakuna, śakuni, suparṇa, śyena* and the evil sound of *śakumas* i.e. birds. e.g. *Av.* 10.3.6 states : शकुनेः पापवादादयं मणिः वरणो वारयिष्यते ।

Also *Av.* 19.8 mentions the word *suśakuna* in the mantra : स्वस्तितं मे सुप्रातः सुसायं सुदिवं सुमृगं सुशकुनं मे अस्तु । (*Av.* 19.8.3) But from the context it is clear that the word *śakuna* here stands for 'bird' only.

There are good many references to good as well as bad omens in Sanskrit literature. It is not the case that they are restricted only to birds. The ominous animals even include the human beings as there are beliefs related to the birth of twins etc. (e.g. *Apastamba Śrautasūtra* 2.14.23 states that the birth of a pair of twins requires a special sacrifice because it forbodes evil—childlessness if the twins are human and want of cattle if they are calves.)

Not only this but pages have been written on the

interpretations of omens and steps to be taken to ward off the undesirable future happenings indicated by them. To mention some of the prominent texts that discuss the issue : *Adbhuta Brāhmaṇa*; 13th chapter of *Kauśika Sūtra (KS)*; some portion of *Aitareya Brāhmaṇa*; some parts of the *Av*; many chapters in *Avpariśiṣṭa* etc. are a few and also the works like *Bṛhatsaṁhitā* and *Rājataraṅgi ṇi* discuss it elaborately. There also are works like *Śakunadīpaka, Śakunasāroddhāra, Śakunaparīkṣā, Śakunapradīpa, Śakunārṇava* and so on which deal with this subject independently. Some of these works treated augury as a science (*Śakunaśāstra*) and made it an object of systematic study. Whether it (augury) really is a Science or not may be difficult to ascertain but these works bear the testimony of the fact that augury was studied in India even from that point of view. In other words, attempts were made to systematise the development of the concept.

However, for this paper, I have confined myself to some of the references that are supposed to be oldest ones. Similarly, keeping in the line with the theme of the seminar I have chosen a few 'living omens' and have tried to show their Ancient Indian sources as it is not possible to cover all the references in such a small paper. I am aware that for obtaining the whole idea of living omens and customs related to them one should conduct a survey of villages or less-educated communities where one may find much more information about the present status of the concept.

What is a Śakuna

If a question is asked 'what actually is an omen?' The answer should be, in my opinion, it is a kind of an extra-normal phenomenon. The 13th chapter of *KS* defines it (in the very beginning) as : लोकविरुद्धं दृश्यते तदद्भुतमित्युच्यते। *Adbhuta* is another word for *śakuna*. Thus, it is nothing but some uncommon phenomenon interpreted by the experts or fortune-tellers by various means best known to them. There are various types of omens such as : natural phenomena like *ulkāpāta, vidyutpatana* etc; signs by birds and animals; dreams; human beings; inanimate things and so on. There have always been additions to the list in *Purāṇas*, the Epics and later literature. But the point I wish to make here is that probably, in India, the oldest type of omen was in the form of birds and some peculiar sounds of them or say, their language. The references from

Saṁhitās, that we have seen before, show that the Vedic people sincerely believed that birds have some supernatural powers to know the future and they indicate it through their appearance or various sounds i.e. may be their own language which is not known to the human beings at large. This is the reason why Vedic seers prayed to the birds to think good about them and speak auspicious things about them. In my opinion, most probably, this is why the words denoting a bird namely *śakuna* and also *śakuni* came to denote the meaning 'omen' later on.

Some Living Omens

If one thinks of omens' status today then one will have to accept that though one tries to be rational and not to believe in such type of irrational things, the influence of the tradition and convention is so immense that it becomes a difficult job for one just to forget that the black cat had crossed his way when he was about to begin his journey. In villages or in the areas where education has scarcity value various types of omens might be extant and some rituals or remedies to avoid the evil in future also might be in vogue there but in the big cities of modern times or in the areas where education is vastly spread omens find a smaller place but not no place.

Generally, the seeing of a *bhāradvāja* bird is a good omen.

Crossing of the road by a cat from left to right is a bad one.

Owl and its hooting both are considered bad and indicative of some unfavourable future happenings.

Howling of a dog is without any doubt considered to be an evil omen.

If a crow caws in front of somebody's house it is indicative of coming of guests to that person. It is also considered bad if the cawing of crows is heard at night.

Perceiving a *kākamaithuna* is an evil omen.

Sources

From the above mentioned the first one is referred to in the Ṛv. if the *kapiñjala* of the Ṛv is to be taken as *bhāradvāja* of these days, on the line of our discussion before. There it is not said explicitly that it is a good omen but the bird is called *sumaṅgala* as well as *bhadravādin* and is requested to be auspicious to the people. The desire of its protection is also expressed in *Rv* 2.42 as we have seen before. All this elaborately imply that it is a good omen. The hooting of an owl is directly referred to in the *Rv* 10.165. The seer of the hymn prays to the lord that may what the owl expresses by its hooting turn out to be fruitless or untrue. It is obvious from this that from the time of *Ṛv*. up to the date owl is considered to be an evil omen in India. There are also references to the *kapota* bird (a pigeon) as a messenger of death or ill luck in the *Ṛv*. All the while the seers pray that let the bird be auspicious for us and let it speak favourable about us. At present, however no such concept of good or bad omen is connected with this particular bird i.e. a pigeon.

The cawing of crows if heared at night is considered bad in the *Kau Gr.* (5.5) as we have seen before. The *TS*. 3.2.6.2 refers to a touch of a black bird (possibly a crow) as a bad omen. It seems that a crow is many a time, if not always, considered to be an evil omen.

There is probably no reference to the crossing of way by a cat in the *Vedas* but so far as my knowledge goes there are ample references to this in the *Purāṇas*. it is mentioned there that if a cat passes from right to left of the road then it is a favourable omen whereas opposite of this is bad. In the *Brahmavaivartapurāṇa* cat is mentioned as a good omen which Akrura saw when he went to bring Kṛṣṇa with him. The same belief is there in the minds of people even today.

No direct reference to the howling of a dog as an evil omen could be found. *Sāmrājyalakṣmīpīthikā* records that if a dog bites a person that indicates destruction of wealth (vide : pp. 80-85).

Watching *kākamaithuna* is considered bad in the *Ṣaḍ. Br.*

It may take some more pages to go through the details of these and to add many other omens to the list like *pallisaraṭapatana, kapotapraveśa, piṅgalāsvara, kākavaikṛta, madhuvalmīkotpatti, grāmyāraṇyādimṛgapakṣivikāra* and so on. But this paper aims at just reckoning to the importance and possibility of such a study.

Conclusion

At the very outset I would like to make it clear that the paper does not proclaim the validity of the concept. Actually, we can observe that on account of being fallacious the number of omens is gradually reducing in the more educated communities. My contention is only this that the concept forms an interesting object of a serious study.

If we go to the root of it, we may find that curiosity and fear are two prominent feelings that haunt human mind about the future. Both these are the outcome of the desire to peep into one's own future which is yet to come. In such a situation if an extra-natural phenomenon is observed, it gives the food to the worried mind and it starts interpreting the same to its utmost capacity—thinking that it leads to the knowledge of future. Thus, it is the earnest desire to know one's future before hand that rules over. But this, in my opinion is restricted to the realm of mind only, because when it comes to the brains the whole building is shattered into pieces. Whatever the mind may have in mind the brains cannot make anything out of it since cause-and-effect relationship does not have any footing in the whole business. The concept just cannot stand rationality. Hence I said that it is almost beyond dispute in the rational community that it does not hold any water. Even here we have to add 'almost' because the rational animals are gifted also with minds and at some weak times are governed by them.

It so happens sometimes that two particular incidents occur in a certain order and hastily the preceding one is taken to be the cause of the other, and if the same is repeated at some other time by *Kākatālīyanyāya* (this is known as fallacy of False Cause or Post Hoc ergo Proper Hoc, in modern Logic) it as though becomes a rule and thus the omens come into existence. The cause-and-effect relationship formed on the basis of a few instances is apparent one i.e. fallacious and not real one. But as I said before the worried mind does not stop to think over it and the concept continues to be there. And whether the intellectuals desire or not it will so continue as long as there are weak and worried minds. To conclude, it is an eternal conflict between the rational brains and the emotional minds!

References

1. *Ṛgvedasaṁhitā* with *Sāyaṇabhāṣya*, Vaidik Samshodhan Mandal, Pune, 1936.
2. *Atharva Vedasaṁhitā*, Ed and Tr. S.D. Satavalekar, Svadhyay Mandal, Pardi, 1960.
3. *Taittirīya Saṁhitā* of *Kṛṣṇa Yajurveda*, Ed. S.D. Satavlekar, Svadhyay Mandal, Pardi, 1983.

4. *Śatapatha Brāhmaṇa* with *Vedārthaprakāśa* of *Sāyana*, Jñāna Publsihing House, New Delhi, Reprint 1987, Vol. I.
5. *Aitareya Brāhmaṇa*, Ed. S.K. Pillai, Trivandrum Skt. Sr., 176, University of Travancore, 1955 (Vol. III).
6. *Ṣaḍviṁśa Brāhmana* with *Vedārthaprakāśa* of Sāya a, Ed. B.R. Sharma, Kendriya Sanskrit Vidyapeeth Sr., 9, Tirupati, 1967.
7. *Aśvalāyana Gṛhyasūtra*, Ed. V.L. Palshikar, J.M. Pustakalay, Bomaby, 1909.
8. *Apastamba Śrautasūtra*, Ed. A. Shrinivasaraghavacharya, Oriental Research Institute, Sanskrit Series, 104, Mysore, 1960.
9. *Kauṣītaki Gṛhyasūtra*.
10. *Kauśika Sūtra* of *Atharva Veda*; Ed. M. Bloomfield, Motilal Banarsidass, Delhi, Varanasi, Patna, 1972.
11. *Nirukta* of Yāska, Kshemaraj Shrikrishnadas, Bombay, 1912.
12. *Atharva Vedapariśiṣṭa (The Pariśiṣṭas of the Atharva Veda)*, Ed. G.M. Bolling, Chaukhamba Orientaila, Varanasi, 1976.
13. *Sāmrājyalakṣmīpīṭhikā*, Tanjore Saraswati Mahal Series, No. 58, Saraswati Mahal, Tanjore, 1952.
14. *Dharmasindhu* of Kashinath Upadhyay, Reprint, Satguru Publications, New Delhi, 1986.
15. *Encyclopaedia of Religion and Ethics*, Ed. James Hastings, Edinburgh, T and T Clark, 38, George Street, 1911, Vol.IV.
16. *Vaidikakosha (Viṣayon evam nāmon kā)* (Hindi) by Suryakant, Benares Hindu University, 1963.

14

Attitude and Feelings of Man Towards Nature as Reflected in *Dharmagranthas*

Many a time it is pointed out that as knowledge advanced, many sciences grew independent of each other in the West. It did not happen so in India. Well, it is true. Our books on Logic contain Philosophy of a very high order, they also touch upon many psychological issues, they also provide theories of creation and so on. In the West, however, Philosophy, Logic, Psychology, Cosmology are developed as independent sciences if I may say so. But I think it is here that we are different from others. It is a fact that our ancient literature is a treasure-house of various gems of thought and the beauty of this treasure lies in the fact that these gems of thought are closely connected with each other as if woven in a string in a fascinating manner.

Accordingly, our *Dharmagranthas* are basically the books of laws of conduct but they also reflect many aspects of human life simply because the authors of these texts have prescribed the rules and regulations only after studying and taking into account all the aspects of human living. And environment being an important factor for human well being, awareness about it is also found in these texts. Of course, it goes without saying that these are not the text books on environmental science and hence one will not get the materials on environment as scientifically as the environmental science may demand today. Nevertheless, there is difference between environmental science and environmental awareness. Science of environment is something different that being aware, being alert about one's environment. We, here, are to discuss the latter one. And there are certain references to the same. In this line, I have tried to highlight some points by interpreting certain references found in the texts on *Dharmaśāstra*. The scholars are to decide whether I have read too much between the lines. For this paper I have confined myself to the *Gautama Dharmasūtra, Viṣṇu Smṛti,* Hemādri's *Dānakaṇḍa* of *Caturvargacintāmaṇi, Nirṇayasindhu* of Kamalākara Bhaṭṭa and *Dharmasindhu* of Kāshināth Upādhyāya only.

While describing the feelings and attitude of these people towards surrounding nature that includes animals, trees and insects etc. also along with the five *mahābhūtas* namely, *pṛthvi, ap, tejas, vāyu* and *ākāśa,* I have chosen to speak about their attitude towards animals and trees in particular. While doing so, I may give some other relevant references as well. It is not the case that they have something to say about each and every aspect or element of environment. It is also not the fact that they do not have anything to say about nature. They definitely have many things to say about it which show their awareness.

That Hindu religion and culture show close association with nature is not a new piece of information. There is no doubt about it. On the other hand, our sciences and philosophies and almost all branches of learning are influenced to a great extent by religion and culture. Hence whatever they have said may loosely seem to be said from purely religious point of view, but one will never be able to prove that something has been said from only such and such point of view. Well, one never knows. Here, our real task is to find out the relevant passages and think of the possibilities behind them in which those particular statements are made. Take, for example, a statement from *Viṣṇu Smṛti (VS)* :

ब्राह्मे मुहूर्ते उत्थाय मूत्रपुरीषोत्सर्गं कुर्यात्। ...न अप्रच्छादितायां भूमौ। न फालकृष्टायाम्। न चोषरे। न शाद्वले। ...न पथि। न रथ्यायाम्। न उद्याने। न उद्यानोदकसमीपयोः। न गोव्रजे। न आकाशे। नोदके। (*VS*.60. 1-24)

(Translation) : One should leave his excreta getting up early in the morning. He should not leave it on an uncovered land, not in the field, not on the unploughed ground, not on the lawn, not in the street, not on a small road, not in the garden, not near the garden or water-reservoir, not in the cowpen, not in the air or space, and not in water-reservoir.

Now, we cannot, without doing injustice to the statement say that this is stated merely from religious point of view. If the action is taken up as per this *Smṛti-statement,* it will play the role of preventing pollution to the air and water in spite of its performing all possible religious duties. Is it reading too much between the lines? Well, I do not know. But I would say this : When there are more than one possibilities say, ways and places for performing an action and one among them is particularly prescribed, one can infer that the law giver is aware of what and why is he enjoining.

To turn to the main theme of the paper, the paper is divided into three parts : (1) Attitude and feelings towards animals, (2) Attitude and feelings towards trees, and (3) Conclusion.

(1) Attitude and Feelings Towards Animals

The tendency of elevating the natural elements to the level of gods and deities is as old as the *Ṛgveda*. In the *Ṛgveda* the deities like Uṣas, Savitṛ, Varuṇa, Agni, Parjanya are well known. The same tendency is found in the *Dharmaśāstra*-texts also. They have prescribed worship of various animals on various days of an year. *Nirṇayasindhu* (p. 146-47) has prescribed *govatsapūjā* as follows : कार्तिककृष्णद्वादशी गोवत्ससंज्ञा। सा प्रदोषव्यापिनी ग्राह्या। and further says, सवत्सां तुल्यवर्णां च शीलिनीं गां पयस्विनीम्। चन्दनादिभिरालिप्य पुष्पमालाभिरर्चयेत्।।

Similarly, bulluck-worship, serpent-worship etc. which are observed even in this age were prescribed by our *Dharmaśāstra* texts. In other words, they have deified these animals.

One might wonder what has it got to do with the environment? After all what is our environment? The sum and total of all these factors. What is the purpose behind this deification? If we think a bit more the implication will become obvious. It is as follows : Once you treat something as a deity, you will simply worship it lest harm or destroy it. Thus, deification is no doubt religious but the result of it is the harmony with and balance in nature by keeping the animals etc. intact.

They were aware of the fact that balance in nature is necessary for the happiness of human being. Look at the following verses which depict the feeling of gratitude towards the dumb animals for their service to the mankind.

उत्पाद्य सस्यानि तृणं चरन्ति तदेव भूयः सकलं वहन्ति।
न भारखिन्नाः प्रवदन्ति किञ्चित्, अहो वृषैर्जीवति जीवलोकः।।

(*Skandhapurāṇa* quoted by Hemadri in the 7th chapter of *Dānakhaṇḍa*).

Tr : They produce the crops and eat (only) grass. They bear all the burden and never complain about it. The world lives because of the bullucks.

पुरा निर्मितवान् ब्रह्मा वृषभं धर्मरूपिणम् ।
or प्रजां धरत्ययं भूमौ धर्ममूर्तिवृषो यत: ।

(*Brahmapurāna* quoted by Hemadri in the 7th chapter of *Dānakhaṇḍa*)
Tr : *Brahma* created the bulluck, the *Dharma* incarnate. or

He sustains the subjects on the earth and hence he is *Dharma* personified.

The same feeling of gratitude is expressed towards cow also.

तृणानि खादन्ति वसन्त्यरण्ये पिबन्ति तोयान्यपरिग्रहणि ।
दुह्यन्ति वाह्यन्ति पुनन्ति पापं गवां रसैर्जीवति जीवलोक: ।।

(*Skandhapurāṇa* quoted by Hemādri, ibid)

Tr : They eat grass, live in the forests, take water not belonging to anybody. They give milk, carry the burdon, purify the sins, people live on their milk.

न वधार्थं प्रदातव्या न कीनाशे न नास्तिके ।
गोजीवे न च दातव्या तथा गौ: पुरुषर्षभ ।।

(*Mahābhārata* quoted by Hemādri, ibid.)

Tr : A cow should not be given for killing, not to a plough-man, not to a skeptic and not to a person who earns his livelihood by her means.

There are many more references on this line which amply show their feelings towards animals. Of course, this does not mean that animal-killing was totally prohibited or non-vegetarian food was condemned—no. But their basic principle was, 'do not kill animals without any reason.' This attitude is reflected in the following statements :

पक्षिजलचरकृमिकीटघातनं जलजसूदनं फलेन्धनकुसुमस्तेयमित्येतन्मलिनी-

करणम् उच्यते । (*Gautama Dharmasūtra pariśiṣṭa* 2 6.6) - Gautama has given the list of sins in which he counts : Tr : killing of birds, acquarian animals, insects, animals born in water is a sin. Similarly, stealing the fruits, fuel or flowers is a sin.

Look at this one :

द्यूतं हीनसेवाम् अदत्तादानं हिंसा च परिवर्जयेत्।

(*Gautama Dharmasūtra* 1.2.23.)

Tr : One should avoid playing dice, serving a lower person, stealing and *hiṃsā* i.e. killing. Here commentator has interpreted this word *hiṃsā* as killing or torturing the animals (Vide Maskari's comm. on the above passage). Viṣṇu has also given a big list of sins in which he treats ग्राम्यारण्यानां पशूनां हिंसा संकरीकरणम्। (Tr : The killing of the tame and wild animals) as a sin and also 'पक्षिणां जलचराणां जलजानां च घातनम् कृमिकीटानां च। इति मलावहानि' 'Tr : Killing the birds, acquarian animals, animals born in water, insects etc. is a sin (Vide *Viṣṇu Smṛti* chapter 39 and 41). Viṣṇu has prescribed expiatory rites and also punishments for the killers of the animals like मूषक (mouse), मार्जार (cat), नकुल (mongoose), मण्डूक (frog), सर्प (snake) and also for a killers of birds like शुक (parrot) क्रौञ्च (cranes), तित्तिरि (partridge) etc. There is a big list of birds and animals in this context (vide *Viṣṇu Smṛti*, ibid).

Almost all the rules stated above are of *arthavāda*-type which ultimately aim at the refrainment of man from taking up those particular acts.

Another interesting ritual demonstrates the feelings of man towards all his fellow-beings. The name of the ritual is *Bhūtayajña* (sacrifice for beings). This rite is to be performed by the householder every day. The following *mantras* stated by the *Śudrakamalākara* sufficiently speak of the implication behind this ritual.

देवा मनुष्या पशवो वयांसि सिद्धा सयक्षोरगदैत्यसङ्घाः।
प्रेताः पिशाचा तरवःसमस्ता ये चान्नमिच्छन्ति मया प्रदत्तम्।।
पिपीलिकाः कीटपतङ्गकाद्या बुभुक्षिताः कर्मनिबन्धबद्धाः।
प्रयान्तु ते तृप्तिमिदं मयान्नं तेभ्यो विसृष्टं सुखिनो भवन्तु।।

Tr : Let the gods, men, animals, birds, ascetics, *yakṣas*, reptiles, demons, departed souls, ghosts, trees and all those who are desirous of food offered by me, ants, insects and flies etc. who are hungry and tied up by the fruit of their deeds, be satisfied with the food offered by me and be happy.

(2) Feelings Towards Trees

As in the case of animals, trees like *Vaṭa* (Banyan tree), *Śami* (a tree possessing a very tough hard wood) and *Bilva* (wood-apple tree) are also deified. Similarly, the invariable relation between a particular tree and a particular deity is also well known to us. Deification of trees or their close associations with the deities and gods certainly elevate the trees to a higher level and thence the feelings towards them are also disclosed.

They have treated trees as sentient beings. A verse from the *Mahābhārata*, quoted by Hemādri runs as follows :

स्थावराणां च भूतानां जातयः षट् प्रकीर्तिताः ।
वृक्षगुल्मलतावल्लयस्त्वक्सारास्तृणजातयः ।।

(Hemādri 13th chapter)

Tr : There are six species of immobile beings, namely, tree, bush, creepers, bamboo trees and their class and the class of grass.

Some times the *mantras* that are uttered at particular times depict the feelings in their mind effectively. Look at this verse from the *Nirṇayasindhu* :

बिल्ववृक्ष महाभाग सदा त्वं शङ्करप्रिय ।।
गृहीत्वा तव शाखं च देवीपूजां करोम्यहम् ।।
शाखाच्छेदोद्भवं दुःखं न च कार्यं त्वया प्रभो,
गृहीत्वा तव शाखां च पूज्या दुर्गेति च स्मृतिः ।।

(*Nirṇayasindhu, Saptamīpūjāvidhiḥ*)

Tr : O sir, Bilva tree, you are always dear to the Lord Śaṁkara. Taking your branch I now worship the goddess (Pārvatī). Please bear the pains of cutting your branch.

It is obvious from this that he is fully aware of the pains he is causing to the tree by cutting its branch. It is also noteworthy that the tree is addressed as lord.

Plantation of Trees

Dharmasindhu has prescribed proper time for the plantation of trees (*Vṛkṣāropaṇakāla*).

Hemādri observes in the *Dānakhaṇḍa* of his *Caturvargacintāmaṇi* that a person who is unable to give even a pot of water in *dāna*, should water the *Aśvattha* regularly. He will shake off all evils and will beget good progeny :

उदकुम्भप्रदानेऽपि ह्यशक्तो यः पुमान् भवेत् ।
तेनाश्वत्थतरोर्मूलं सेच्यं नित्यं जितात्मना ।।

(13th chapter of *Dānakhaṇḍa*)

अश्वत्थरूपो भगवान् प्रीयतां मे जनार्दनः ।

This is the *mantra* that he has to utter while watering the tree. Now look at this verse. Hemādri quotes Yama :

कूपारामप्रपाकारी तथा वृक्षस्य रोपकः ।
कन्याप्रदः सेतुकारी स्वर्गमाप्नोत्यसंशयम् ।।

(13th chapter of *Dānakhaṇḍa*)

Tr : One who digs a well, makes a garden one who provides a place of drinking water for travelers, one who plants a tree, or one who gives his daughter in marriage, one who constructs a bridge (over a river) goes to heaven (after death) no doubt.

Such sentences may seem to be made from only religious point of view prima facie. But, if we think twice it may be said that it is evident from all such references that these people have felt the nerve of the then-society, that was-probably-more afraid of the unseen results (*adṛṣta*) of their deeds than the seen ones for obvious reasons. Hence, if it is said that one will obtain heaven by taking up such and such activity he will obey the statement instantly on one hand and without any additional effort he is benefited in this world on the other.

Hemādri has quoted many verses in the praise of the trees and their plantation from the *Mahābhārata*. To state some of them :

अतीतानागतौ चोभौ पितृवंशौ च भारत ।
तारयेद्वृक्षरोपी च तस्माद्वृक्षांश्च रोपयेत् ।।
पुष्पैः सुरगणान् वृक्षाः फलैश्चापि तथा पितृन् ।
छायया चातिथींस्तात पूजयन्ति महीरुहाः ।।

पुष्पिताः फलवन्तश्च तारयन्ति परत्र च ।।
पुत्रवत् परिपाल्याश्च पुत्रास्ते धर्मतः स्मृताः ।।

(13th chapter of *Dānakhanda*)

The import of these verses is as follows : One should plant the trees and look after them just as one looks after his own son because the trees oblige us by their flowers and fruits as well as they offer their shade to the travelers.

Similar verses are also quoted by Hemādri from many *Purāṇas*. While quoting Viṣṇu, Hemādri says in the 13 chapter of *Dānakhaṇḍa* :

वृक्षारोपयितुः वृक्षाः परलोके पुत्रा भवन्ति । वृक्षाः प्रसूनैर्देवान् प्रीणयन्ति, फलैश्च अतिथीन् । छायया अभ्यागतान्, देवे वर्षति उदकेन पितॄन् ।

There is another quotation from Vṛddhagautama :

वृक्षच्छेत्ता वृथा यस्तु स नाडीव्रणवान् भवेत् ।
वक्ष्यामि तत्प्रतीकारं सर्वलोकहिताय तु ।।

(13th chapter of *Dānakhaṇḍa*)

Tr : One who cuts the trees without any purpose suffers from various diseases. Let me tell the expiation for that for the well-being of the whole world.

Here, the word सर्वलोकहिताय is the most important one. Cutting of trees has to be prevented for the well-being of all—this is the implication.

It can be said from all this that for avoiding cutting of trees or making harm to them i.e. for all practical purposes they either deified them or established emotional relationships with them.

Look at the verse from *Matsyapurāṇa*, quoted by Hemādri in this context :

दशकूपसमा वापी दशवापीसमो द्रुमः ।
दशद्रुमसमः पुत्रः दशपुत्रसमो द्रुमः ।।

(13th chapter of *Dānakhaṇḍa*)

Here, it is obvious, that a son and a tree are treated at parwhen he says ten trees are equal to one son and ten sons are equal to one tree.

How a tree is adopted as son is described in *Skandapurāṇa, Brahmavaivartapurāṇa, Nandipurāṇa, Matsyapurāna* etc. also in the *Dharmasindhu* under the name *taruputravidhiḥ*. Not only this, *Dharmasindhu* has described *upanayana* of *Aśvattha* and we all know that Tulasi-vivāha is observed even today.

3. Conclusion

From whatever is discussed above, it can be concluded that may be these people were not facing the same problems that we are facing today. Nevertheless problems were there in those days and they were fully aware about them and knowing the root-causes of them had taken care to root those very cause out. For example, today's pollution problem is mainly caused by industrial waste, automobile exhaust and population. But, the household wastage, excreta of human beings and animals, dead bodies etc. were there to be disposed off even in those days, and we have seen that these were taken care of properly.

They are also aware of the fact that trees have an important role to play in the human well-being hence they prescribed the plantation of trees and prevented cutting of trees without reason by prescribing various punishments. The way by which they achieved this was their own and which they perhaps thought to be most effective. If at all they sound religious, it was necessary to achieve the desired result to which I have already hinted.

A book entitled, 'Know Your Environment, by G.K. Seth defines Environmental Engineering as follows : "Environmental Engineering is that branch of Engineering that involves the application of scientific principles to the prevention, control and management of environmental factors that may influence the physical and emotional health of man and his well-being."

Now, Environmental Engineering is a branch of Environmental Science which has such a big scope and Environmental Science is the main tree which actually should encompass the area of almost anything everything related to our environment, and environment includes everything that surrounds us, including ourselves.

Now, let us analyse our data in brief. All the references to the deification of animals and trees show that the man was aware of his close relation with the nature and was interested in protecting all the elements of the nature. Here, deification is not important but the purpose behind it is significant. The purpose is to refrain man from any type of harm or disrespect towards these elements of the nature of which the man himself is one part. One can easily notice that many of the rules and laws mentioned above are of *arthavāda*-type. Purpose of *arthavādas*, by definition is something other than what they express. Here it is obviously refraining the human beings from the destruction of the nature.

The references to the plantation of trees from the *Mahābhārata* and *Purāṇas* quoted by Hemādri are rich with their environmental awareness. By establishing emotional relationships with these elements, they have tried to compel man to preserve this treasure of natural wealth. This is Environmental Awareness.

When Viṣṇu prohibits the excretion near water reservoir, in the air, in the gardens, the green lands etc. with all other possible purposes in his mind, he is helping avoid pollution caused by these things to air and water all the same.

Let us conclude with the verse of *Brahmavaivarta Purāṇa*, quoted by Hemādri (13th chapter of *Dānakhaṇḍa*) which is capable of becoming a motto for the propagation of plantation :

पुत्रैर्विना शुभफलं न भवेन्नराणाम् ।
दुष्पुत्रकैरपि तयोभयलोकनाशः ।।
एतद्विचार्य सुधिया परिपाल्य वृक्षान् ।
यत्नेन वेदविधिना परिकल्पनीयाः ।।

References

1. *Gautama Dharmasutra* with Maskari's Commentary, Ed. by Veda Mitra, Mitra and Sons, Karol Bagh, New Delhi, 1969.
2. *Gautama Dharmasūtra Pariśiṣṭa*, The Adyar Library Series, No. 64, Adyar, Madras, 1948.
3. *Viṣṇu Smṛti*, Ed. by J. Jolly, The Chowkhamba Sanskrit Series, No.95, Varanasi-1, 1952.
4. Hemādri's *Dānakhaṇḍa* of *Caturvargacintāmani*.
5. *Nirṇayasindhu* of Kamalākara Bhaṭṭa.
6. *Dharmasindhu* for Kāshinatha Upādhyāya, Reprint, Sri Satguru Publications, Shakti Nagar, New Delhi, 1986.
7. *Know Your Environment* by G.K. Seth, National Publishing House, 23, Darya Ganj, New Delhi, 1979.

15

Freedom of Women and Manu

It is quite well known and well accepted a fact that Manu did not grant much freedom to women or that he was not in favour of the independence of women. From the oft-quoted verse, *'pitā rakṣati kaumāre bharatā rakṣati yauvane'* (Manu 9.3) or the verses like, *'asvatantrāḥ striyaḥ kāryāḥ puruṣaiḥ svaiḥ divāniśam'* (Manu 9.2) the above mentioned fact becomes quite evident. P.V. Kane in his history of *Dharmaśāstra* observes : In the *Dharmaśūtras* and Manu, women is assigned a position of dependence and even women of higher classes came to be looked upon as equal to *śūdras* so far as Vedic study and several other matters were concerned. Manu 9.3 says that women have no independence and in all stages depend upon men.[1]

Thus, this and all other verses of *Manusmṛti* concerning women and their status in the society speak of the general outlook of Manu on this issue. Nevertheless it also remains the fact that there are verses like, *yatra nāryastu pūjyante remante tatru devatāḥ yatraitāstu na pūjyante sarvāstatrāphalāḥ kriyāḥ*, (Manu 3.56) or *śocanti jāmayo yatra vinaśyaty āśu tat kulam*[2] which are from the same pen of Manu. Moreover, there are some statements like, *arakṣitā gṛhe ruddhāḥ puruṣaiḥ āptakāribhiḥ, ātmānam ātmanā yās tu rakṣeyuḥ tāḥ surakṣitāḥ* (Manu 9.12) and a few more which need due consideration.

The aim of this paper is, thus, to point out some of the exceptional type of statements which may reveal some deeper layer of Manu's mind that thought about women who had to face some uncommon situation. After examining these statements we shall try to draw some conclusion regarding Manu's opinion about the status of women.

Accordingly, the paper is divided into four parts :

1. The exceptional rules concerning the marriage of girls
2. The exceptional rules concerning the women whose husband is away on journey

3. The rules concerning the widows
4. Conclusion

(1) The Rules Concerning the Marriage of Girls

While stating the proper time of marriage of girls, Manu says : A girl should be given in marriage before she attains puberty, because otherwise her father will be a sinner.[3] He further says that one should seek a bridegroom for his daughter who is an excellent man, good looking and a perfect match for his daughter.[4]

These two are the general rules. It is quite understandable that all people do not have same circumstances i.e. same facilities and same amount of favourable conditions and so on. To explain, there is every possibility that in some case there would be some difficulty in following these above mentioned rules due to the lack of the favourable conditions. What does it mean? Let us think of a situation where a father, in spite of his willing to give his daughter in marriage, is unable to get a proper match for his daughter. Now here the question arises, whether he should bear the sin of not giving his daughter in marriage at a proper time, or he should give his daughter to any Dick, Tom or Harry to avoid that sin.

Manu's answer to this question is : *Kāmamā maraṇāt tiṣṭhet gṛhe kanyartumatyapi, na ca ivenām prayacchet tu guṇahīnāya karhicit* (Manu 9.89).

This opinion of Manu, according to me, is very important. Here setting aside his own principle and all the so called social bindings Manu straight forwardly states that in such a situation there is no harm even if the daughter stays at her father's house until her death. But in no case should the father give his daughter to an unworthy match.

Let us think of some other situations. Suppose, there is nobody to look after a girl or to search a husband for her. Here again the question arises : What should the girl do? Is she given freedom to seek a husband for herself or she has to remain unmarried the whole life? In such a situation Manu says : *Triṇi varṣāni udīkṣeta kumāri ṛtumatī satī, ūrdhvan tu kālād etasmād vindeta sadṛśam patim* (Manu 9.90).

(2) The Rules About the Women Whose Husband is Away on Journey

Now let us turn to the statements in connection with the women whose husbands are on journey. The basic rule in this context is meant for men. Manu says, whenever a man goes on journey for some work he should provide his wife with sufficient amount of money for her necessities. Because otherwise there is a possibility of her falling to an error.[6]

Manu further states, when the husband is on journey and he has provided his wife with all necessary things, his wife should remain faithful to him.[7]

Now there is every possibility that some man may go on journey without giving the sufficient amount of money to his wife. In such cases what is the duty of that woman? Manu says : *proṣite tv avidhāyaiva jīvec chilpair agarhitaiḥ* (Manu 9.75) 'She should maintain herself or sustain her life with honourable means of livelihood.'

The general rule of Manu himself is, a woman is always dependent on a man. He clearly opines that either her father or her husband or her sons protect her.[8] But still, when an uncommon situation of the type mentioned above arises he directs the women to live with self-respect.

Another statement in this connection is, *Proṣito dharma-kāryārtham pratīkṣyo' ṣṭau narah samāḥ vidyārtham ṣaṭ yaśortham vā kāmārtham trīn tu vatsarān* (Manu 9.76). A woman should wait eight years for her husband who is on journey for some religious purpose, six years if he is away for learning or to acquire fame and three years if he has gone to marry another girl.

This statement of Manu implies that if a woman marries some other person after the above mentioned period, she is not at fault.[9]

Thus, though it is a general rule laid down by Manu[10] that under all circumstances a woman has to serve, honour and be faithful to her husband, in the cases mentioned above Manu clearly allows a woman to marry again.

(3) The Rules Concerning the Widows

Now let us see the statements of Manu pertaining to the widows. General rule in this connection says that a woman should not betray her husband after his death. She should not utter any other man's name[11] or she should not go to any other man either to acquire her livelihood—or for the purpose of having a child.

Manu says, if she observes *brahmacarya* after her husband's death then she will obtain heaven even if she is childless.[12]

These are the general rules in this context. Manu condemns the tendency of woman's going to some other man after her husband's death.

But let us imagine the following situation : A woman becomes widow in the prime of her youth. She is left without a son and she does not want to die. In such a situation[13] who is going to support her? What should she do? Here Manu speaks about the *niyogavidhi*. What is a *niyogavidhi*? If a woman desires a child, as a support to her, she may have it from her brother-in-law if allowed by the elderly persons.[14]

Thus, it is clear from this that even though Manu condemned *niyoga*[15] in normal circumstances, he himself allowed it to be observed in some particular situation. It is quite evident from this that he does not want to bar women's fundamental right to live.

(4) Conclusion

The following are my observations on all the cases and relevant rules or statements of Manu discussed above :

Manu was really not in favour of the women's freedom in general. But he did not deny the fact that there could be some complicated or extra normal circumstances where all his general rules could not be applied in toto. Or if applied they will not prove to be meaningful, but they may prove to be detrimental to women's welfare. And so, he made some exceptional type of rules which could be observed in those extraordinary situations.

We can clearly see from the verse *kāmam ā maraṇāt tiṣṭhet* etc. (Manu 9.89) that Manu did not want to do any injustice to women by prescribing some rigid and harsh rules. From the statement of Manu namely, *trīṇi varṣāṇi* etc. (Manu 9.90) we can say that Manu granted certain amount of freedom to women to choose their husband when they are well grown up and have to find their own way out.

Looking at the rules that he states about the *proṣitabhartṛkās* we can easily feel that he has taken into account all the possible situations that might have arisen in those days.

In the modern times these rules may seem to be insignificant but they definitely bore much importance at the time they were laid down.

In case of widows also though he states that the ideal position of the widows is to observe *brahmacarya* after their husband's death, still he thinks of some adverse situation and lays down the *niyogavidhi*, even though it is not appreciated by himself to be nice in some other situation.

In short, the verse
pitā rakṣati kaumāre
bhartā rakṣati yauvane etc. (Manu 9.3)
Reflects the actual status of women in the then society of the time of Manu. But it can be observed from what we have discussed so far that nowhere the humanitarian outlook has been sacrificed by Manu. The exceptional rules bear testimony to this fact. There is no doubt that Manu wants women to have protectors in the form of either father, or husband, or son all through in all stages of their life, but at the same time he wants that a woman should not be put to any disgraceful state of life.

One may find apparent contradictions in his statements, but if all the contradictions are read together with the conditions or situations in which those appear, it will not be difficult always to find grounds for those apparent contradictions. Mostly, those cases of contradictions may appear to be exceptions to the general rules.

References

1. *History of DharmaŚāstra*, P.V. Kane, Vol.II, part I, Govt. Oriental Series, Class B. No. 6, BORI, Pune, 1941, p. 367.
2. *Na Śocanti tu yatraitā vardhate tad hi sarvadā Manu*. 3.57.
3. *Prayacchet nagnikām kanyām, ṛtukālabhayānvitaḥ/*
Rtumatyām hi tiṣṭhantyām eno dātāram ṛcchati Manu. 9.88.
4. *Utkṛṣṭāyābhirūpāya varāya sadṛśāya ca*
Aprāptām api tām tasmai,
kanyām dadyāt yathāvidhi // Manu. 9.73.
5. *Mātṛkam bhrātṛdattam vā*
stenā syād yadi tam haret / Manu. 9.92.
6. *Vidhāya vṛttim bhāryāyāḥ*
pravaset kāryavān naraḥ /
Avṛttikarṣitā hi strī
Praduṣyet sthitimaty api // Manu. 9.74.

7. *Vidhāya proṣite vṛttim jīven niyamam āsthittā / Manu.*9.75.
8. *Bālye pitur vaśetiṣṭhet*
   pāṇigrāhasya yauvane /
   Putrāṇām bhartari prete
   na bhajet strī svaiantratām // Manu. 5.148.
9. The commentator of *Nandinī* observes :
   Urdhvam bhartrantaraparigrahe na
   doṣo'stīty abhiprāyaḥ /
10. *Viśīlaḥ kāmavṛtto vā guṇair vā parivarijitaḥ /*
    Upacaryaḥ striyā sādhvyā satatam devavat patiḥ // Manu. 5.154.
11. *Na tu nāmāpi gṛhṇiyāt*
    patyau prete parasya tu / Manu. 5.157.
12. *Mṛte bhartari sādhvī strī*
    brahmacarye vyavasthitā /
    svargam gacchaty aputrā'pi yathā te brahmacāriṇaḥ // Manu. 5.160.
13. In the words of Manu, *Ataḥ param pravakṣyāmi*
    yoṣitām dharmam āpadi Manu. 9.56.
14. *Devarād vā sapiṇḍād vā*
    striyā samyag niyuktayā /
    Prajepsitādhigantavyā
    Santānasya parikṣaye // Manu. 9.59.
15. *Guruniyogāt apatiḥ apatyalipsuḥ devarāt*
    gurupreritāt ēyāt ītyāgamaḥ /
    Tantravārtika of Kumārila Bhaṭṭa on 1.3.3.7

16

Duties and Rights of Women in the *Yājñavalkya-Smṛti*

There are two altogether different outlooks among people in our society regarding the issue of status of women in the society. One of them straight away decries all the *Dharmagranthas*—especially the *Manusmṛti* for the *smṛtikāras* have been partial in this matter according to them. This out-look is based mainly one the popular verses of Manu like *na strī svātantryam arhati (Manusmṛti*, 9.3) which are seldom understood in proper context. The other one upholds the opinion that the position of women was (and perhaps this group of people claims, it is so even today) very high and they are honoured by all. This opinion is based mainly on the verses like *yatra nāryas tu pūjyante, ramante tatra devatāḥ* again from the pen of Manu (*Manusmṛti*, 3.56).

In my opinion both of these are two extremes—which may be far from the actual fact. The fact may be lying somewhere in between these two extremes.

We, in this chapter, are mainly concerned with the 'duties and rights of women in the *Yājñavalkya-Smṛti (YS)* and their relevance, if any, today.'

When we talk about the rights and duties and women or their status in our society, generally, the above mentioned verses of *Manusmṛti* and some other verses like,

शोचन्ति जामयो यत्र विनश्यत्याशु तत्कुलम्।
न शोचन्ति तु यत्रैता वर्धते तद्धि सर्वदा।।

(*Manusmṛti*, 3.57)

come to our mind, as they are well known to us. The reason behind this is on one hand Manu is a very popular author among all the *smṛtikāras* and on the other he is very elaborate while dealing with any issue. He has also described the rights and duties of women in his *saṁhitā*, quite at length. From his text we do get a general idea regarding the status of women in the then society.

When we come to Yājñavalkya, we find that he is very brief and precise as compared with Manu. He has, no doubt, prescribed rules for women in all the main stages of life—i.e. for (1) married women, (2) women whose husband is on journey, and (3) widows.

From this classification itself it is apparent that a woman had to be designated as either a wife of a husband who is staying with her or as of a traveler or of him who is dead i.e. woman did not have any other way of existence or reference than that she is a wife of somebody. Rather her status depended on the status of her husband. In the then society marriage of a girl used to take place when she was at the most 10-12 years old. This is the reason why while prescribing the duties for women the law givers start with a married woman as her duties start after marriage only.

With this background, let us now see how Yājñavalkya deals with this issue. One thing I would like to make clear here that Yājñavalkya has not classified these rules but the classification is done by me for the sake of convenience of discussion.

Duties of Married Women

Yājñavalkya says : स्त्रीभिः भर्तृवचः कार्यम् एष धर्मः परः स्त्रियाः।
आशुद्धेः सम्प्रतीक्ष्यो हि महापातकदूषितः।।

(*YS*, 3.77)

Tr.: Women should keep their husband's word as this is the highest duty of a woman. If, in case, however he has committed a *Mahāpātaka* (great offence) then she should wait so long as he is purified (by an expiation).

The expression *āśuddheḥ sampratīkṣyo* in the verse is explained by the commentator of *Mitākṣarā* as—she need not depend upon him in that period and when he performs the expiatory rites and gets purified she should again obey him and depend upon him as before.

There is one more verse in this context which is an *arthavāda* —type and which may be considered as an advice to a woman. It runs as follows :

मृते जीवति वा पत्यौ या नान्यमुपगच्छति।
सेह कीर्तिमवाप्नोति मोदते चोमया सह।।

Tr : A woman who does not love any other man (than her husband) no matter whether her husband is alive or not, obtains great fame in this world and she enjoys the company of Umā (by the influence of her merit) in the other world.

The duties of women are prescribed in these two verses. There are some verses which may depict the right of women indirectly. Indirectly because these rules are addressed to men and not to women.

Rights of Women

सकृत्प्रदीयते कन्या हरंस्तां चोरदण्डभाक्।
दत्तामपि हरेत्पूर्वाच्छ्रेयांश्चेद्वर आव्रजेत्।।

(*YS*, 3.65)

Tr. : A daughter is given (in marriage) only once. Giving her once to a person if her father gives her to someone else then he should be fined like a thief. But if the second person (*vara*) is a better choice then the father should do so (i.e. he is not at fault.) *Mitākṣarā* adds here that this can be done before the marriage is solemnized—*etacca saptamapadāt prāk draṣṭavyam*.
Now look at the following verses :

सुरापी व्याधिता धूर्ता वन्ध्याऽर्थघ्न्यप्रियंवदा।
स्त्रीप्रसूश्चाधिवेत्तव्या पुरुषद्वेषिणी तथा।।
अधिविन्ना तु भर्तव्या महदेनोऽन्यथा भवेत्।
यत्रानुकूल्यं दम्पत्योस्त्रिवर्गस्तत्र वर्धते।।

(*YS*, 3.73 and 74)

Tr. : A person should remarry if his wife is such who takes liquor, who is suffering from an ailment, one who is cunning, who is barren, who wastes or destroys money, who speaks harsh words, who gives birth to female children and one who hates her husband.

When he so marries, he should take care of her food otherwise he would be committing a great sin. Actually, where husband and wife live in harmony—there all the three (namely—*dharma, artha* and *kāma*) prosper.

There is one more verse about the remarriage of a man :

आज्ञासम्पादिनीं दक्षां वीरसूं प्रियवादिनीम् ।
त्यजन्दाप्यस्तृतीयांशमद्रव्यो भरणं स्त्रियाः ।

(*YS*, 3.76)

Tr.: Obedient, alert, who is a mother of brave progeny and who speaks sweet words—if a husband leaves her, then he should give her 1/3 of his wealth. If he is poor then he should take care of her food only.

It is clear from these verses that the intention of Yājñavalkya is that if a woman is not at fault she should not suffer or rather should be taken care of properly. It is well known that at that particular time polygamy was allowed in our society but while stating the grounds for second marriage in the verse *surāpī vyādhitā* etc. mentioned above, Yājñavalkya very much sees that no injustice is done to the woman. In other words, if it is not possible to live with a wife because of the bad qualities of her then alone a man should marry for the second time.

In the list of bad qualities mentioned by Yājñavalkya we may not agree with some cases like *vandhyā* or *strīprasū* etc. today. These cannot be the bad qualities of a woman we know today but at that particular juncture of time in the then society they were considered so probably subject to their social set-up. But one will agree that the bad qualities mentioned by Yājñavalkya excepting these few are the causes of dispute and in many cases that of divorce even today. Because they cannot be liked by anyone at any time—they are eternally bad or undesirable so to say.

Rules for Widows

While stating the rules for widows Yājñavalkya is very brief. The only verse in this connection runs as follows :

पितृमातृसुतभ्रातृश्वश्रूश्वशुरमातुलैः ।
हीना न स्याद्विना भर्त्रा,
गर्हणीयाऽन्यथा भवेत् ।।

(*YS*, 3.86)

This may be translated as follows : A woman should not live without her father or mother or son or brother or father-in-law or mother-in-law when she is without her husband. Otherwise she becomes an object of censure.

This implies that when her husband is absent say, has gone on journey or died she should live with some of her relatives and not alone. If she stays alone she is condemned by the people, which ultimately comes to the main theme that a woman is vulnerable and should be protected by someone in the family—which in turn is not totally unacceptable even today.

Observations

In the rules that Yājñavalkya has prescribed for women, their duties and rights are depicted to certain extent. One can observe that the period of time in which these rules were enjoined was such that women were not allowed to educate themselves and they did not have any other engagement than to look after the household work and the children. In such a situation if they were to live independently i.e. without their relatives they were liable to fall and hence they are advised not to live alone. All other rules also could be understood properly in the same way i.e. by keeping the time and social set-up in mind in which they were written.

Needless to say that no man or woman from an educated community would like to call all these rules relevant today and would incline to follow them in toto. But at the same time there is some element of truth in them which nobody could deny even at present times. For example the rules enjoined for *proṣitabhartṛkā* are followed to a great extent even today though the women following them are not aware that they are following the instructions of say Manu or Yājñavalkya or any other *Dharmaśāstrakāra* for that matter. We i.e. modern generation comes to know of these things as tradition. Tradition and convention are two important factors that direct us in our life time at many important moments. These traditions and conventions ultimately have their roots in the *Dharmaśāstra* texts which are in turn based on *Dharmasūtras* that have a very big and long background of Vedic culture—rather they are part and parcel of the Vedic culture.

Many things in this tradition may seem useless or irrelevant in modern times as times are changing very fast and science has advanced to a very great extent. But none-the-less, there are certain principles which will remain there for ever—which will be tested on the day's needs time and again, but will never be disturbed or discarded. Because the authors of these texts were not only authors but they were seers who had seen the fundamental essence of human nature and also its flaws and enjoined the rules accordingly. Human nature to a great extent has remained the same through ages and hence many of these rules are still applicable—only the details of them may have changed.

Index